POETRY COMPETITION

GREAT MINDS

Your World...Your Future...YOUR WORDS

From Northern Ireland Vol I
Edited by Donna Samworth

 Young**Writers**

First published in Great Britain in 2005 by:
Young Writers
Remus House
Coltsfoot Drive
Peterborough
PE2 9JX
Telephone: 01733 890066
Website: www.youngwriters.co.uk

SB ISBN 1 84602 079 4

Foreword

This year, the Young Writers' 'Great Minds' competition proudly presents a showcase of the best poetic talent selected from over 40,000 up-and-coming writers nationwide.

Young Writers was established in 1991 to promote the reading and writing of poetry within schools and to the youth of today. Our books nurture and inspire confidence in the ability of young writers and provide a snapshot of poems written in schools and at home by budding poets of the future.

The thought, effort, imagination and hard work put into each poem impressed us all and the task of selecting poems was a difficult but nevertheless enjoyable experience.

We hope you are as pleased as we are with the final selection and that you and your family continue to be entertained with *Great Minds From Northern Ireland Vol I* for many years to come.

Contents

Hayley Elliott (12)	64
Rachel Smyth (12)	64
Elaine Simpson (11)	65
Lauren Hunter (13)	65
Lily Rebekah Sittlington (11)	66
Claire Wilson (13)	66
Catherine Campbell (12)	67
Lisa Douglas (12)	67
Sarah Breen (12)	68
Megan Ferguson (12)	68
Samantha Greenhill (11)	69
Cathy Callaghan (13)	69
Erin Smith (11)	70
Lydia Morrell (11)	70
Chloe Holmes (12)	71
Lynsey Purdy (11)	71
Emily Mesev (12)	72
Sarah McCreadie (11)	72
Amy McConkey (12)	73
Hannah Rankin (11)	73
Shauna Platt (12)	74
Taylar Wilkinson (11)	74
Jordan McCahon (11)	75
Jessica Elliott (12)	75
Zoë McCook (12)	76
Alannah Cardwell (11)	76
Demi Nicolle Black (12)	77
Karen Adams (12)	78
Issy Craig (11)	78
Zara Leighton (12)	79
Rebecca McFaull (11)	79
Emma Jayne Bannister (13)	80
Stacey Tosh (11)	80
Karla-Jayne Stewart (11)	81
Lynsey Adams (12)	81
Gill Arbuthnot (12)	82
Ellen McKinney (12)	82
Meryl Gamble (12)	83

Coleraine Academical Institution, Coleraine

Thomas Kelso-Mason (12)	83
Andrew Cunning (12)	84
Dylan Frew (14)	84
David Harding (12)	85
Simon Clarke (12)	85
Calvin Thompson (11)	86
Philip Gilliland (12)	86
Gavin Kane (13)	87
Jordan Millican (12)	88
David McCluskey (11)	89
Ben Macaulay (11)	90
Matthew Adams (13)	91
Scott Lorimer (11)	92
Niall Adams (12)	93
William Doherty (14)	94
Glenn Elliott (12)	95
Callum McAfee (14)	96
Michael Wallace (13)	97
Tom He (13)	98
Terry Daly (12)	99
Matthew Stavri (11)	99
Stephen Best (11)	100
Nicolas O'Neill (13)	100
Ben Martin (13)	101

Kilronan School (Special SLD), Magherafelt

Tomas Murray (16)	101
Steven McKeever (16)	102

Lisanally Special School, Armagh

Sasha Bingham (11)	102
Sheena McKenna (15)	102
Philip Patton (13)	103
Sandie Gibb (14)	103

Magherafelt High School, Magherafelt

Adam Davison (11)	104
William Davison (13)	104
Helen Hawthorne (12)	105

The Poems

Seeing The Thread

Today upon the empty beach I sat
And tried to see so far away
In the sea I think I may have glimpsed that
Place our eyes are forbidden to stray.
I peered deeper into the waves
But the image that I beheld
Began to sink to Poseidon's floor
And I could not grasp it again.
Daily now I stand by the water and
Try not to trespass to that secret place
But now I regret that I pushed the hand
Which changed the thread by which my life was laced.

Amy Finch (16)

Choose Life

Youth, encouraged to be passionate
Passionate about whatever they feel - race, religion . . .
But too much passion leads to hate
Hate then leads to crime and you have nothing

Youth, encouraged to do something with their lives
Have their way of life paved for them by their elders and senior figures,
Dictating *their* future and stifling their ambition
Allowing them no choice

Youth, the future, your future
Youth, do what you want, when you want, your choice
Do drugs, commit crime, drink, you choose
Choose big screen TVs, dishwashers, fast cars and a flashy lifestyle.

Youth, the choice of wasting away at the end of it all
In an old person's home, watching mind-numbing game shows
Wondering what you've done with your life
Maybe their lives do need to be paved for them!

Youth, your chance,
Your life,
Your choice
Choose life, live it.

Gary Lloyd (17)
Ballyclare High School, Ballyclare

A Poem

Impatience is a vice
of which there is a heavy price,
The best whisky takes at least a score
if you taste others, you'll want no more.

On television, plain to see
adverts rely upon this plea
To take things easy and not to rush
otherwise the brain will turn to mush.

That's certainly not a pretty sight
seen in daylight or at night
This horrific warning's universal
applying even to the household gerbil.

Poems and novels, satire or not
can make the temper really hot,
Creativity requires the time
to give great care to every line.

At the speed a gambler throws the dice
I would dish out this advice,
My friends and colleagues, unless you're able
you had best avoid the writer's table.

Peter Tweed (17)
Ballyclare High School, Ballyclare

Hallowe'en

The nights are getting dark
Put your costume on
It makes the dogs bark
When you sing that Hallowe'en song

'Hallowe'en is coming
And the geese are getting fat
Will you please put a penny
In the old man's hat.'

Knock on a door, trick or treat?
Sweets are on my mind.
Who will I meet?
What will I find?

'If you haven't got a penny
A half-penny will do
If you haven't got a half-penny
Then God bless you
And your old man too!'

The door swings open, what's that sound?
Oh, it's very scary
Quick turn round!
It's something big and hairy!

PS: It's the dog!

Conor Shearer (11)
Ballyclare High School, Ballyclare

Five Ways Of Looking At A Waterfall

The waterfall is like all the rivers joining together.
The water falls and splashes against the flowing stream.
It's like a never-ending story, it just goes on and on.
The waterfall is like the slides at water parks.
It's like a great, big lake.

Amber Victoria Stewart (13)
Coleraine High School, Coleraine

Tom Robinson

(Inspired by 'To Kill A Mockingbird' by Harper Lee)

Here I am, alone in my cell,
I'm waiting and waiting and waiting, but well
Her mean old pa raised the alarm,
I didn't do nuthin', I meant no harm.

What did I do? I defended my honour!
But now I know that I'm a goner.
I couldn't have done it, not with my arm,
I didn't do nothin', I meant no harm.

She's just a girl, not much younger than me,
I hope Mr Finch makes them see,
I'm just a black man who works on a farm,
I didn't do nothin', I meant no harm.

Amanda McIntyre (15)
Coleraine High School, Coleraine

Alone . . .

(Inspired by 'To Kill A Mockingbird' by Harper Lee)

I'm all alone, nowhere to be seen,
It's not my fault they're all so mean.
My heart is kind, I can do no right,
But people remember me by the fight.

I got in some trouble you see,
But I was released, but only me!
They thought it was for the best,
However so far, it's been a test.

I want to step out and have no fears,
And not be discriminated by my peers.
To live a life in which I belong to
And have an identity instead of just Boo!

Victoria Balmer (16)
Coleraine High School, Coleraine

Without Hope!

(Inspired by 'To Kill A Mockingbird' by Harper Lee)

All I do is work hard all day long,
Why do the white folk think that's so wrong?
I always help others, don't ask for nothin' in return
The white folks don't ever learn!

All I did was help the young miss
Thought's being kind, but she wanted a kiss.
I know I'm in trouble now, no road to turn
Still the white folks don't ever learn.

Her daddy's an evil man and she was mistreated
All I did was pity her and now I'm seated
In a cold room, all on my own, waiting to burn
And still the white folks don't ever learn!

Kyla Roxborough (15)
Coleraine High School, Coleraine

The Bogeyman

I am so lonely
And full of strife
Imprisoned in my house
You don't know my life

I have no friends
I am so lonely
People gossip, people talk
But they don't know me

I can still dream
Of the world outside
Sunlight framed in the window
But I may never know.

Naomi Moore (15)
Coleraine High School, Coleraine

Innocence

(Inspired by 'To Kill A Mockingbird' by Harper Lee)

Just a simple man
With a simple old life
Just trying to be good
Not tryin' to be rude

That girl called me in
She needed some help
Then she fell for me
I tried to get free

I'm an innocent man
With an innocent life
I have lost all my friends
And now I've lost my life.

Christine Gilmore (15)
Coleraine High School, Coleraine

Boo

(Inspired by 'To Kill A Mockingbird' by Harper Lee)

Can't go back outside where they hate me,
People here just don't realise;
Sure I'm normal, as anyone else,
Still I see the fear in their eyes.

Lost my freedom, one stupid mistake
People here just don't forgive.
Think I'm insane, going crazy
Still don't have a real life to live.

Given the chance I wouldn't go back
People here still hate me.
Used to the solitude, I accept it,
Still it's sad that no one knows me.

Lynsey Workman (15)
Coleraine High School, Coleraine

It's Tough For A Mockingbird

(Inspired by 'To Kill A Mockingbird' by Harper Lee)

It's tough in these parts
When it's simply black or white
The way honest black men are treated
Is a ridiculous sight

It's tough at this time
And I've worked hard all my life
I'm gonna battle for my rights
In this never-ending strife

It's tough at a trial
My black word against that girl's
It isn't all Mayella's fault though
Her pa's made her mind a whirl

It's tough in my life
I'm stuck in a racist bend
Can Atticus really help?
Oh when will this suffering end?

Lauren Campbell (15)
Coleraine High School, Coleraine

Skin Deep

(Inspired by 'To Kill A Mockingbird' by Harper Lee)

You're not born lucky if you're born black
The white people don't ever cut you no slack
They knew the truth but no one was brave
It didn't bother them If I went to my grave

I was not capable of committing the sin
My arm got caught in a cotton gin
Miss Mayella was sad, Miss Mayella was young
I just wanted to help her some

I never touched her but I haven't a case
I'll be condemned because of my race
Mr Finch tried to help me, he did his part
Never looked at my skin, just at my heart.

Ashleigh Kilgore (16)
Coleraine High School, Coleraine

Boo's Window

(Inspired by 'To Kill A Mockingbird' by Harper Lee)

I've not been out since way back when,
I did some wrong; I didn't know then.
Alone at home is where I lie,
Through glass I watch the world go by.

Got in with a crowd, was led astray,
For the rest of my life I'll have to pay.
Living this way till the day I die,
Through glass I watch the world go by.

As the children pass, they stare at me;
I often fear I'll never be free.
The neighbourhood always squint and pry,
Through glass I watch the world go by.

Hayley Blues (15)
Coleraine High School, Coleraine

Bogeyman Blues

I am the bogeyman everyone fears
No one's seen me in years
Nothing is fair
Trapped in here, my nightmare

Every day I try to be kind
Putting out things for kids to find
Does anyone really care?
Trapped in here, my nightmare

My family are so hard on me
Oh how I wish I was free
Go outside, do I dare
Spring this trap, end my nightmare?

Emma Harkness (15)
Coleraine High School, Coleraine

I'm Innocent For Sure

(Inspired by 'To Kill A Mockingbird' by Harper Lee)

It's tough being black round here,
'Cause I'm livin' in constant fear,
People accuse me of all sorts,
But I'm innocent for sure.

I'll never be acquitted,
But the only crime I committed,
Was feelin' sorry for a white girl,
So I'm innocent for sure.

The trial will be a tough day,
But I've just gotta hope and pray,
That Atticus will try 'n' help,
To find me innocent for sure.

Danielle Brown (15)
Coleraine High School, Coleraine

Where For Eternity?

Life is short, it goes by so fast,
We need to realise it does not last.
It's over in the drop of a hat
But then where, after that?

You know that you're close to the end,
But where, oh where, your soul to send?
You have your family closely sat,
But even where, after that?

Heaven or Hell, which do you choose?
You have everything to lose.
When you're gone and the grave is flat,
But then where, after that?

Clare Laverty (15)
Coleraine High School, Coleraine

Colour

(Inspired by 'To Kill A Mockingbird' by Harper Lee)

Black, pink, red, brown,
All these shades cause white to frown.
We should all have equal rights
In courts, jobs and even fights.

Separate churches, we have no schools
Do we really look like fools?
Do this, do that, come here, go there,
With no respect, it's just not fair.

We are black and they are white
But what if we all had no sight?
What if we all helped each other,
Treated each colour like a brother?

Remember, inside we're the same
Our colour just an outer frame.
And sometime, somewhere you will see
The world will live in harmony.

Emmaline McCollum (15)
Coleraine High School, Coleraine

Serenity

The water laps gently against my feet,
in a gentle calming beat.
Wrapped in the warm air,
I'm without a care,
I sit in the tiny bay,
forgetting my thoughts of the day.

The stars twinkle so bright,
the sky is a glorious sight.
Pinks and oranges can be seen,
where the sun previously had been.
If the world were as calm as this sea,
wouldn't it be a better place to be?

Rebecca Oliver (14)
Coleraine High School, Coleraine

The Sea

Gently rippling, beautifully shimmering,
The delicate waves lap against the rocks.
Placidly drifting, silently skimming,
Dark green seaweed glides towards the docks.
Beaming sunshine, atmosphere calming,
The tranquil day smooths out all anxiety.
Golden sun setting, darkness falling,
Day ends so peacefully and radiantly.

Angrily smashing, furiously swirling,
The sea spits and sprays in every direction.
Winds howling, rainfall pounding,
Dark storm clouds in formation.
Viciously chilling, constantly shivering,
All warmth and happiness stolen away.
Waves battering, savagely lashing,
Such a contrast to earlier in the day.

Hannah Stevens (15)
Coleraine High School, Coleraine

Two-Tones

(Inspired by 'To Kill A Mockingbird' by Harper Lee)

A town together but so divided,
A split of race that society decided,
Everything in black and pure white,
These colours determine what's wrong and what's right.

The whites so flawless but false, insincere,
The blacks who live in a prison of fear.
The only colour accepted is white,
But which of the colours determine what's right?

Exceptions are made for black and white,
On both, some are good and others are slack,
So look at these colours with a different light,
Are either the colours the one that is right?

Lisa Wilson (15)
Coleraine High School, Coleraine

Wow!

I sometimes think I'd like to be
An Olympic star that sails the sea
But now I've found something new,
It even comes equipped with shoes!

Watchful eyes, excited sighs,
Before me lies a sea of flags,
What direction should I go?
Naturally, my dear . . .
Go with the flow!

As I look up I plainly see
A floating silken stage for me.
Away! Away! My desires arise,
Toil and trouble was worth the sacrifice.

Up from the river, dark and deep
I urge my oars to make a sweep.
Power and peace is flowing now
I felt so good - I could take a bow.

In the shadows down below
Close by the edge of the river
Something's moving, very slow.
I glanced around, it made me shiver,
I drop the paddles in the silver thread
I'm starting now to lose my head.

Go
Faster and faster, I tore along
My hands are sore
It won't be long.
I stroked the river, without a splash,
Over the line.
Home at last!

Stephanie Boomer (15)
Coleraine High School, Coleraine

Friends

A friend is a gift you give yourself
And nothing can come between true friends.
Good friends are good for your health
There's nothing a true friend wouldn't do.

Most people deserve their enemies but
Friends deserve their friends
Friends know all about you and still like you
The friends will stick by you till the end
But true friendship is given to a very few.

Friendship is one heart in two bodies
You can't live with them, can't live without them
No one is whole because your friends will always
Be a part of you
A friend is the purest of all God's gifts.

Katie Leighton (14)
Coleraine High School, Coleraine

The Ground Thunders

The ground thunders,
A mass of legs and dust,
Muscles ripple under their skin,
With a glossy coat of silk,
Powerful necks bow to the gods,
With flowing, silky hair,
Which is buffeted by the wind,
They have galloped for centuries,
And helped the development of the world we know,
They have been companions, workmates and a solace,
Ladies and gentlemen, I present to you . . .
The horse.

Laura Kirk (15)
Coleraine High School, Coleraine

Contrast Between Autumn And Summer

There is a nip in the air
the days are shorter,
Carefree sunny days are past
long, still, clear evenings have gone.

Crimson crisp carpet of leaves
pumpkins, conkers and apple pies,
Bees are silent, butterflies have vanished
buckets and spades are packed away.

Rockets, Catherine wheels screaming into the night sky,
wrapped up children by fires,
Ferris wheels are still,
ice cream vans silent
Summer has past, autumn is here.

Laura Campbell (14)
Coleraine High School, Coleraine

Five Ways Of Looking At A Snowflake

A snowflake forms and its shiny white surface
Twinkles through the sky.

A snowflake symbolises a cold, frosty winter's morning
Where all I want to do is snuggle in my bed.

A snowflake is like a dancer who elegantly floats under the clouds,
Gracefully twirling around.

A snowflake is like a small piece of white,
Fluffy cotton wool.

Where a snowflake falls to the ground,
It melts and slowly fades
Like a person drifting into a deep sleep.

Laura Doherty (13)
Coleraine High School, Coleraine

The Bandersnatch

(Inspired by 'Jabberwocky' by Lewis Carroll)

The Bandersnatch is very tall,
His arms are very thin.
His legs are not so very small
Unlike his younger kin.

He ruffles through the tulgey night,
Tell me, are you scared?
Did he give you such a fright,
To make you spiky-haired?

He snips your locks with his scissor-hand.
Never be on your own.
The woods, they are his private land
Where he can range and roam.

If you escape him, lucky you
No more evil to see.
He will make you into mince stew.
You escaped, 'Hee, hee, hee!'

Clare Taylor (12)
Coleraine High School, Coleraine

Food

For those of us who love our food
The future does not look so good
It seems that what we love to eat
Should only be a sometimes treat.
Chocolate fudge cake, cheese and chips
They may put inches on our hips
But life would only be a trial
To live it full of self denial.
Instead of something quite obscene
I really should be eating greens!
But I would give up all of them
In favour of my Midget Gems.

Hannah Farthing (15)
Coleraine High School, Coleraine

Fire

Cunningly stalking its prey
It creeps up without a warning
It has no mercy on its victim
Devouring it in a whirlwind of smoke and flames.
Sparks angrily spurt high into the heavens
They dance playfully, full of life
It gains ferociousness and power
Becoming wild with excitement,
Untameable, it runs free
Beautiful yet deadly.
Powerful and magnificent
Its flame's like a mane
The oranges and red spurt out.

Becoming calmer it plays gently
The long fingers of colours twisting and turning
They come back down to the ground
Specks of light jump out from the centre
Softly crackling and growling
Daintily flickering in and out
It dies down, slinking away silently
Leaving behind a savaged mess.

Alice Harpur (15)
Coleraine High School, Coleraine

Winter

The winter snow glistens white,
The days turn quickly into night.
The trees sway, brown and bare,
Almost like they've lost their hair.
The sea is not blue, instead it's grey,
To match the cold and cloudy day.
Children play until their cheeks are red,
They moan and groan when it's time for bed.

Janine McCaw (15)
Coleraine High School, Coleraine

Peace

Peace is a place where time stands still
It seems oh so perfect and great, until
A crash or a bang disturbs this place
Causing destruction for all to face

Peace is a place of laughter and fun
To sit around and lounge in the sun
But peace is not all it's cracked up to be
Because someone will spoil it, like you or me

Peace is destroyed in this wonderful place
And it's all down to the human race
If we don't care for this wonderful gift
It will simply cease to exist

So put down your guns and stop the fighting
Instead pick up a pen and start writing
So you can tell others of your superb choice
And help build a peacekeeping voice

My poem has a meaning and that's why I'm writing
To keep the peace and combat the fighting
I've done something about it and so should you
So now all that's left is, what should you do?

Ashleigh Taylor (15)
Coleraine High School, Coleraine

Bonfire Night

Bonfires smoke and burn all night,
Eager trick or treaters, their faces painted white,
The stars and moon hidden with smoke,
Children love it, just one big joke!
Bonfire Night's over, everyone's sad,
Except my dog Sooty, he's very glad.

Tabitha Kee (11)
Coleraine High School, Coleraine

Changing

Selfishness and pride
Take over our lives,
Easy to get
And hard to accept.

Do you consider others
Or are you just not bothered?
The rich and the poor
Do you just close the door?

Maybe if you could only see,
The real depth of humanity,
All might change for you
And for me.

Let us forget the past,
And make changes fast,
Turn around and see
A better me.

Fiona Allen (14)
Coleraine High School, Coleraine

Winter

He bites your toes
With his frost,
And sprinkles snow everywhere.
He's cold and dark
Small and skinny,
And has hair like a grizzly bear.

He seems so scary,
But is quite sweet,
He brings you presents and things to eat.
Although he's scruffy
And leaves frost on the ground.
We still have Christmas to look forward to
The whole year round.

Suzanne Fillis (14)
Coleraine High School, Coleraine

A Cold Caress

The wind is beating against my face
Like a thousand knives,
The rain jabbing my bare legs
And drowning my school bag.

The frost has frozen my lips
The ice is gathering on my fingernails,
I glance at the graveyard
Wishing I could lie in the warm and inviting Earth.

A car whizzes towards me
And screeches to a halt.
Splattering me in muddy brown water
A car door opens to reveal my mother.

How grateful I am when I sit in the heat
And when my sister passes me a towel.
I snuggle into its soft surface
And slowly, slowly drift into sleep.

Rebecca Jayne Farmer (11)
Coleraine High School, Coleraine

Blueberries

A petite and circular berry
That is the colour blue
Is filled with bitter, blood-red nectar
Which is also quite sweet too.
The smell of this small berry
Is a rich aroma which many adore.
Once you've eaten the first one
You will want to come back for more.
Everything I've told you is so very true,
So maybe when you eat them
You will like them too.

Ymelia Stevenson (13)
Coleraine High School, Coleraine

My Green Apple

The shiny green skin
Gleaming in the light
The sweet juicy smell
What a delight!

The hard core inside
Not nice to eat
But the taste of the apple
Is really a treat!

The bittersweet taste
Is really quite nice
It's not like a mixture
Of sugar and spice!

I love a green apple
To finish my tea
A nice Granny Smith
Mmm - that will do me!

Hannah Hough (14)
Coleraine High School, Coleraine

So Sweet!

The sweet smelling scent of a summer's day,
Displays the colours of a sunset and glowing embers.
Soft to touch, like newborn skin,
The tender skin breaks, I can resist no longer,
So sweet! My nectarine.

Tastebuds explode! As the juices run freely,
Savour each delicate bite,
I wish this could last forever,
As I reach the heart, so full of new life.
So sweet! My nectarine.

Jenni Crossley (13)
Coleraine High School, Coleraine

A Peach

A peach is soft and fluffy
With a smooth and fleecy feel,
If you gently massage its skin
This makes it easier to peel.

It smells tropical and fruity
It also smells so sweet
And when you sink your teeth in it
It's really such a treat.

Inside it's yellow, smooth and juicy
Then in the centre, an oval stone
With veiny threads of brown and red
This stone's pitted like a chewed dog's bone.

The skin of a peach is very pretty
Orangy-yellow, and blushing pink
Like a beautiful sunset and rosy cheeks
That's my analysis, what do you think?

Sarah Acheson (14)
Coleraine High School, Coleraine

Recipe For A Perfect Friend

Begin with bags full of laughter
This will make the mixture solve any problems.
Add a teaspoon of helpfulness
And an ounce of love.
Mix with care
For added spice.
Next stir in the style
Or attitude
In order to have a good friendship.
Bake for years
And serve with happiness.

Rachel Millar (11)
Coleraine High School, Coleraine

Friends

Friends to me mean a lot,
When I've met them, they won't be forgot.
The only way to have friends is to be one,
Friends make you laugh; with your friends you have fun.

Special people you can rely on, people who are kind,
These are the memories that won't be left behind.
Thoughtful, honest, picking you up when you're down,
Some of the qualities you will have found.

When you're sad, they'll dry your tears,
When you're scared, they'll comfort your fears.
When you're worried, they'll give you hope,
When you're confused, they'll help to cope.

This is what some people mean to me,
Friends forever, they'll always be.
Sticking beside you, as if like glue,
What exactly do friends mean to you?

Laura King (14)
Coleraine High School, Coleraine

The Red Grapefruit

My grapefruit is red,
It's got a distinctive taste,
And it's soft as a bed,
It's as smooth as paste.

Bright on the inside,
Segmented and juicy,
Dull on the outside,
Thick and not juicy.

It's firm but tender,
It has thick skin,
Nice in a blender,
But don't eat the skin, it goes in a bin.

Zoë Campbell (13)
Coleraine High School, Coleraine

Kiwi

Small and oval,
Tough and greenish-brown,
With hairs like eiderdown,
This is my exterior look.
Soft and green,
Succulent and seedy,
And as juicy as a gumdrop,
This is my interior look.
Bitter and tarty,
Mild and fading,
Mouth-watering for sure,
This is what I smell like.
Tangy and tender
Taste bud tingling,
That's tantalisingly delicious.
That is what I taste like.
With hairs that feel fine,
A hard white core inside
And seeds that crunch between your teeth.
What am I?

I'm a scrumptious kiwi fruit.

Nicola Stirling (14)
Coleraine High School, Coleraine

Eight Ways Of Looking At A Cloud

A cloud is a visible mass of water vapour floating in the sky.
Sometimes light, velvety and silky.
Sometimes masses of smoke or dust meandering aimlessly.
Often like a white fleecy coat of fluff.
Reminds you of cotton wool buds attached together.
Looks like sugary candyfloss.
Also looks as soft and feathery as my pillow.
A cloud is like a sheep with no head or legs, drifting across the sky.

Nicola Bacon (14)
Coleraine High School, Coleraine

VIII Ways Of Looking At A Clock

Its nimble hands strike twelve,
Its day has begun.

Like a musician counting beats
The pendulum swings,
As if a metronome.
It whiles away the seconds.

Its pale shiny face
Has been framed by numerals
Twelve disciples,
Twelve separate eras.

Without time,
No beginning,
No end.

There is never enough time,
But time is never-ending.

Watch the hands travel
Round and round.
Time is not a solid, liquid or gas,
So how can it fly
Or slip away?

A dying man stares at the clock,
Wishing for time to stop
To fulfil his dreams.

When our time on Earth is over,
When the Earth's time is over,
Time still lives on,
It is eternal
Only no one will be around to hear its
Tick-tock.

Sarah Boyd (14)
Coleraine High School, Coleraine

Nine Ways Of Looking At Clouds

Big puffs of fluff,
Soft, delicate and light.
Magically floating about with ease,
In a carefree flight.

Huge, white whales,
Swimming gracefully,
Through the vast, glistening ocean of sky.

Choking, fluffy foam,
Exploding from the fire extinguishers,
Drowning out the flames of the sun.

Elegant, little, white fairies,
Prancing way up high,
In an unknown world up there in the sky.

Suddenly without warning!
They turn into an ugly, angry mob!
Charging across the sky,
Crashing into one another in mad fury!

Black, dark stallions,
Galloping across the moors,
Wild and free.

Then they sob down tears,
Big droplets that had been locked up for so long,
Finally freed.

Mighty roars soon erupt,
Like that of a lion from the cloud's core,
Here comes the thunder!

Great, gold knives,
Stab the Earth and brighten the sky,
Sending flashes and shocks around,
And leave somebody to die.

Estelle Cheuk (14)
Coleraine High School, Coleraine

Six Ways Of Looking At The Sky

At night it's a blanket of darkness
Keeping us nicely tucked in.

The tiny stars shine so bright
Twinkling and glistening at night.

The moon guides us with its great light
It brightens up our night.
It looks like a ball of cheese
So tasty, can I have some please?

In the day the sky looks like the ocean,
Keeping separate from the real one,
If it fell it wouldn't be fun,
Splashing on us all weighing a ton.

The fluffy clouds are like little creatures
Moving swiftly onwards
So many shapes that don't stop
Just keep going on forwards.

The sun's like a great fire
Stuck up there in the sky.
Though it can't burn anything
Because nothing goes up that high.

Annie Hegarty (14)
Coleraine High School, Coleraine

Happiness And Sadness

Misery and despair surround you,
Everything is going wrong.
Life's not worth living
The world's against you.

You feel like you're flying,
You are free.
Nothing can stop you,
You can do anything.

Catherine Lamont (14)
Coleraine High School, Coleraine

Four Ways Of Looking At A River

As it flows in the morning at daybreak,
Like a loose ribbon weaving
Through different shades of green and yellow
Grass like luscious velvet stitched to the rolling meadows.

The sun rises and shines on the calm water
Reflecting all the surroundings on its surface,
A never-ending, true mirror image,
Of all that lives on its banks.

As the tide changes, it starts to rush and babble,
Meandering through the weeds and rushes,
Like the rushing commuters
On a London subway.

When nightfall comes,
The bright moon shines, turning the river into the sky.
Here and there, dabs of glitter like stars shine,
Now motionless, once again until dawn.

Holly McCullough (14)
Coleraine High School, Coleraine

World Of Colours

Red, orange, green and blue
The world is painted for me and you.
The fluffy sheep are white
Dotted through the luscious green grass
All for me, one wee lass!
The sky is blue
The road is grey
The sun shines throughout the day.
The moon and stars glow at night,
Shining out their reflected light.
Red, orange, green and blue
The world is painted for me and you.

Kathryn Lynch (15)
Coleraine High School, Coleraine

Six Ways Of Looking At The Sun

The sun is a
Great ball of fire in the sky

It's like a large, orange basket
That's got caught in the sky

The sun lights up our world like
A bulb lights up a room

The sun was a symbol
For people years ago

The sun is represented
With happy times

If a child is happy,
They are said to be sunny
I'm sunny.

Kathryn Smyth (14)
Coleraine High School, Coleraine

Envy

Envy is a tall, young woman,
With long, straight, black hair.
Her emerald-green eyes are piercing.
She wears a flowing green dress,
With a long apple-green cloak.
She sweeps along with such grace,
Looking and envying everyone she sees.
As a little girl
She was always teased and called mean names
And she wished she was different.
She then started to envy
Everyone who, in her eyes, was perfect.

Lauren Kettyle (13)
Coleraine High School, Coleraine

A Kiwi

The hairy skin,
The rough gruff feel
The refreshing taste
So what's the deal?

It looks so ugly
But tastes so sweet
The lime-green colour
The dots so neat

The riper the fruit
The softer to feel
The symmetrical pattern
Within the peel

The nicest fruit
Ever grown
Is the kiwi
I'd never moan

About the exotic
Taste on my tongue
Scooping the flesh
Is so much fun!

Gillian Simpson (13)
Coleraine High School, Coleraine

Laughter

Laugher is a bubbly sensation that tingles in your tummy
Laughter is a bittersweet sugar treat that is terribly yummy
Laughter is an infectious disease, you catch it like a bug
Laughter isn't just any disease; it's like a great big hug
Laughter is the one thing the world can't do without
Laughter makes the world turn round without half a doubt.

Anna White (12)
Coleraine High School, Coleraine

Seasons

The golden summer days are over,
I am stripped of my freedom, as the trees are of leaves,
Dark evenings draw near, black as a witch's cat,
And then before we know it, Hallowe'en is here.

Seven long weeks hang ahead,
No time to rest one's weary head.
The days run like clockwork, week after week,
No one seems to care that we are beginning to weep.

Christmas comes and laughter too,
I was so happy just to spend time with you.
Giving and receiving, a time of goodwill,
'Not for much longer,' said I, before returning to school.

The puddles have gone, the sun reappears,
Lambs are in the glistening green grass.
Daffodils are blooming and birds are singing,
Suddenly things aren't so bad.

Just one more day to go,
The clock ticks slowly by.
Everything is so perfect,
As I look out the window and sigh.

Summer's here at last!
I'm free for two more months.
Long glorious summer evenings too,
To spend, just with you.

Louise Rowan (14)
Coleraine High School, Coleraine

Five Ways Of Looking At A Door

A block of solid wood.
A way to another world.
A way to block out rooms in a house.
A barricade to keep you safe from harm.
A window with no view but the grain of the wood.

Gemma Webster (14)
Coleraine High School, Coleraine

Homework

Who invented homework?
What did they do that for?
We already do enough in class,
Why do they give us more?

We get back home at 4,
We all want to be free!
We want to put our feet up,
And watch a little TV.

We work hard all day,
And we deserve a rest!
If they give us too much to do,
We won't do our best!

Teachers have heard the excuses
And think they are all poor.
'You have to do it on you own!'
What on earth for?

There is one thing,
That might change my view.
They should pay us overtime,
Wouldn't that suit you?

Grace Dickey (12)
Coleraine High School, Coleraine

The Stars

The stars are like little diamonds scattered across the sky.
The stars twinkle like millions of tiny jewels.
The stars are like mini lamps shining in the pitch-black sky.
The stars are as bright as the light on top of a lighthouse.
The stars are like little fireworks bursting in the sky.
The stars look like someone has sprinkled a tub of glitter
over the darkness.
The stars peep out of nowhere as if it is a game.
The stars sparkle and flash as if they are dancing with each other.

Victoria McQuilkin (14)
Coleraine High School, Coleraine

Star Child

(Dedicated to the memory of my star child)

My friend died when I was small
I cried into the night
My tears rose to a waterfall
And gave the stars a fright

I understand now why she went
But simply cannot see
How glimmers of life sent
Did not last for her as for me

She never walked in other lands
She never made a daisy chain
She never thought of other plans
Is there somebody to blame?

I think she was a special one
Who only stayed a while
She left to join the moon and sun
And in the stars I see her smile.

Orla Chapman (12)
Coleraine High School, Coleraine

Anger

Anger is a tall handsome man,
Cheeks are blood-like, fiery red.
Vermilion overcoat sweeps to the floor,
Curly hair on a fireball head.

Squinting eyes are small and round,
Scarlet lips with bloody tinge.
Crooked teeth that twist and point,
A deadly scowl to make you cringe.

Lives alone, no family or friends,
In a house that's dreary and cold.
The crimson wallpaper is peeling from the walls
And the furniture is covered with mould.

Helen Dobbin (13)
Coleraine High School, Coleraine

Sweet Dreams

One night I had a dream
That I was in a bowl of cream.
There were strawberries on top
But then that dream just had to stop.

Then I had another one
I was eating a big, sweet bun.
The bun was so shiny it looked polished
It's a pity that dream was finished.

In the next dream I was with my mates,
We were in a tub of 'After Eights'.
The air was minty and clean
But that dream ended. Oh how mean!

I finally woke up after all these dreams,
And I felt like I had to scream.
It came to morning and at last
I could have all these foods for breakfast.

Julie Allison (12)
Coleraine High School, Coleraine

Road Rage

As you get in the car and drive down the road,
You get so mad at 'L' drivers going too slow.

You rant and rave, scream or shout,
'Just put the foot down and drive around the roundabout!'

Many 'ragers' of the road get so obsessed,
Some use guns, knives or colourful language,
It's enough to make anyone depressed!

If only we took chill pills to calm our frustration,
Or for many young learners, it may result in meditation!

Driving with fury can result in crime,
So 'ragers' of the road, back off and calm down!

Helen Aiken (14)
Coleraine High School, Coleraine

Holidays

I love holidays
Just sitting in the sun
Nothing else to do all week
But join in all the fun.

I love to swim
In the great, big pool
But sometimes my brother
Acts like a fool.

I love the parks
And all the rides
But my favourite
Are the water slides.

Down at the beach
I love the green sea
Even though my toe
Feels like a frozen pea.

The sea might be cold
But the sand is roasting
And where are my mum and dad
Lying toasting?

Everyone thinks
That the food is nice
But I just live on
Chips and rice

Lotions, potions
My mum has them all
Ointment if we're burnt
Plasters if we fall!

Hannah Fillis (12)
Coleraine High School, Coleraine

Summer

I stand for my bus,
On this cold autumn day,
The summer has gone,
And it's another school day

The summer was great,
I had fun with my friends,
We played on the beach,
Wishing it would never end.

We went on a sunny holiday,
Relaxing without care,
We enjoyed it very much,
Why couldn't we stay there?

Summer may be over,
And we may have to go to school,
But I know now that next year,
The summer will totally rule!

Helen Stewart (12)
Coleraine High School, Coleraine

Have Faith In A Friend

A friend is someone you can trust
Put your faith in if you must!

Special times we'll never forget,
Though sometimes we might get upset.

They're always trustworthy, clever and funny
They make my days both happy and sunny.

A friend is someone you can trust
Put your faith in if you must!

Friends, you know are always there
And friends, you'll find will always care.

Stacey Blues (13)
Coleraine High School, Coleraine

Awake

A cold winter's night,
The moon, crisp and bright,
I lie awake,
In the dark of the night.

I can hear no sound,
But rubbing from the ground,
I lie awake,
In the dark of the night.

Smoke darts from my walls,
And fills my senses,
I lie awake,
In the dark of the night.

The fire is blazing,
Lights are flashing,
I fall asleep,
As the dawn sets in.

Caoimhe Burnett (12)
Coleraine High School, Coleraine

Badminton

Badminton is my favourite sport
I love playing on the court.
Badminton is great, it's so much fun
Especially when I have won.

A serve, a smash, a drop, a clear
Now the end of the rally has got to be near.
It's match point, I have to stay calm.
I can feel the sweat coming out of my palm.

I serve the shuttle high, she hits it back
Now I'll try and get on the attack
I smack it down, hard and strong
Boy, that match was really long!

Rachel Huey (12)
Coleraine High School, Coleraine

The Stars

As I look up and gaze at the bright, luminous stars,
I think of sparkling diamonds twinkling in the black
Velvet coat of the night's sky.

Stars are like shiny raindrops caught behind a
Dark barricade bursting to be free and flying.

Like a fresh black-paved driveway covered in beautiful
Glistening snowflakes that appear from nowhere.

Looking up, I think of a million silver coins delicately
Scattered across the dangerous, dark sky.

The shiny sugar granules have disappeared by dawn,
The stars and moon are not there now,
We know that night has gone.

Hannah Breadon (13)
Coleraine High School, Coleraine

The Jubjub Bird

(Inspired by 'Jabberwocky' by Lewis Carroll)

The Jubjub bird has evil eyes,
His neck is long and spindly,
He would give you a scary surprise,
From his cave deep down in Frindly.

He cannot fly very high,
His wings are not so strong,
He can give a sharp sigh,
With his tongue so very long.

He comes out only at night,
He'll chase you so beware,
He is as silent as a kite,
So make sure you take care!

Catherine Stewart (12)
Coleraine High School, Coleraine

Summer's Going!

Summer is happy,
Summer is free,
In summer out come the birds and the bees.
Summer is sunny,
Summer is warm,
Summer is when we put our T-shirts on!
Long walks on the sand, splashing in the sea,
Summer exciting, full of fun and of glee.

Winter is cold,
Summer is not,
Winter is when the sun gets forgot.
Winter is wet,
Winter is chilly,
Winter is when T-shirts look silly!
Winter is when ice goes over the pond,
Winter is when we put our scarves on!

Summer is playful,
Joyful and hot,
And so summer for me
Won't be forgot!

Sophie Robinson (13)
Coleraine High School, Coleraine

Winter Is Here

Winter is here
Winter is here
It's turning cold
And leaves are turning gold
Snow falling
Children calling
Looking out the window
To see the white, bare trees
As we eat sweets out of a tin
Mum scolding, 'Remember to throw your papers in the bin.'
Winter is here.

Victoria Thompson (12)
Coleraine High School, Coleraine

The Jubjub Bird

(Inspired by 'Jabberwocky' by Lewis Carroll)

'Twas dark and the wind did screech and howl,
Through the grimy woods,
Nothing was heard but a distant owl
And its nightly hoots.

Out from the shadows appeared the Jubjub bird,
Squawking as it came,
Its claws are sharp, its feathers are splured,
There's no other bird the same.

Every full moon it comes out to devour
Until the night is gone,
And what it does on its very last hour . . .
Is fly and vanish at dawn.

Rui Wang (12)
Coleraine High School, Coleraine

The Jubjub Bird

(Inspired by 'Jabberwocky' by Lewis Carroll)

The Jubjub bird is extremely fierce
He is ugly, mean and fat
With glowing eyes and razor-sharp teeth
His favourite pastime is eating cats.

He stalks his prey by both night and day
Catching all in his track
Be careful when you go out to play
You might not be coming back.

When it gets dark his call is loud and sharp
His claws are long, his breath is foul
His favourite place to go is the park
Come near his wood and hear him growl.

Lori Shirlow (12)
Coleraine High School, Coleraine

Caterpillar-Butterfly

Tiny caterpillars scuttling along,
Some hairy, some fuzzy, some short, some long.
Different colours, different sizes,
Cute and cuddly, little surprises!

Eating away at the lettuce leaf,
They never stop, they never sleep.
But they have to go away soon,
To sleep inside their little cocoon.

Out they come, after a while,
They no doubt have changed their style.
Legs so slender and delicate
Patterns on them quite intricate.

Butterflies with tiny wings,
Colours of royalty, such beautiful things.
Pretty and perfect in every way,
I think I could watch them all of the day!

Claire McLaughlin (12)
Coleraine High School, Coleraine

Bandersnatch

(Inspired by 'Jabberwocky' by Lewis Carroll)

The Bandersnatch is unlike anything
With squiggly arms and a huge eye
Spends all day in his cave, just chilling
Watching tele with a big sigh

When the day darkens down
He goes out to play
His pretty pink socks turn brown
Jumping in dirt till day

After playtime he goes to bed
Tired of getting dirty
He lays down his sleepy head
Wondering what it would be like to be thirty.

Sarah Robinson (13)
Coleraine High School, Coleraine

The Jubjub Bird

(Inspired by 'Jabberwocky' by Lewis Carroll)

The Jubjub bird is out tonight,
He is creeping around the wood,
He really looks a horrible sight.
He might mistake you for his food.

He listens out for sounds,
He hears the horse go 'Neigh,'
His heart starts to pound
Forever there will he stay?

He doesn't move an inch,
Will he sleep? He might, he might,
Someone gives him a pinch,
He wakes up to the morning light.

Chantêlle Murdoch (12)
Coleraine High School, Coleraine

A Perfect Mum

Begin with bags full of character
This will make the mixture sweet and smell of
the lovely fragrance of lavender.

Add a teaspoon of sugar
And an ounce of spice,
Mix with everything nice
for added girly socials.

Next stir in the pound coins
Or coppers (I prefer the pounds)
in order to be bought clothes.

Bake for 30 minutes.

Then serve with bags full of love!

Amy Brown (12)
Coleraine High School, Coleraine

The Bandersnatch

(Inspired by 'Jabberwocky' by Lewis Carroll)

The Bandersnatch came roaring through,
The forest, still no creature twickled,
He roared, lifted his wings and flew,
Creatures appeared, scared and sickled.

Among them sat a beamish boy,
Frumious, fearful, scared to talk,
No longer was this a game or toy,
Ready and waiting began he to walk.

Towards the lair of the Bandersnatch,
Clutching to his vorpal sword,
At the door he lifted the latch,
He would not go back on his word.

A long time ago on his father's knee
He made a promise for all to hear,
He would slay the Bandersnatch, you'll see,
Without even a hint of fear.

He lifted his sword and brought it down,
On the neck of the fearsome beast,
He turned and went with a victorious scrown,
And on to the celebration feast.

Aimée Hamilton (13)
Coleraine High School, Coleraine

Happiness

Happiness floats like soft clouds in the sky,
Happiness smiles as it walks by.
Happiness brings great joy to the land,
Happiness joins two people by hand.
Happiness is the greatest thing,
That even money cannot bring.

Victoria McAfee (11)
Coleraine High School, Coleraine

Hockey

I love hockey, it is fun
I love it when my team has won
I dribble, run up, try to score
But the other team tries a little bit more

I push on through past the defence
And hit the ball with all my strength
The goalie cannot stop my goal
And all I hear is one great roar

As we pass and play about
Every now and then the captain shouts
'Mark that girl before she scores.'
Every girl is a sweating sore

As time goes on our team is strong
We battle through and dribble along,
The referee, she sounds 'Time's up'
And we have won the Ulster Cup.

I love hockey, it is fun
Especially when my team has won.

Clara Craig (12)
Coleraine High School, Coleraine

Hallowe'en Time!

Hallowe'en has come again,
Bonfires are alight,
Fireworks light up the sky,
Trick or treaters knocking
On your door,
Ghosts and witches
Everywhere,
It's the best time of the year!

Alex Carson (11)
Coleraine High School, Coleraine

Nine Ways Of Looking At The Stars

When darkness comes the night sky shows us the stars,
which could be the suns that are shining down on other
planets in the solar system.

The stars are the white speckles of paint on a black canvas.

They are the lifelong dreams of every living thing.

They are the encouraging guide of those who have
passed on showing us which path to take in life.

They make us feel safe like a protecting, sparkly shield
against all that is evil.

They are tiny, silvery, sparkly insects stuck onto
black Velcro.

They are twinkling little eyes that are winking at us
mysteriously from millions of miles away.

They are tiny fairy lights spread out across the sky like the
ones on Christmas trees.

They are the lights of a large city that go out in the
morning when the sun appears.

Kerry Kilgore (13)
Coleraine High School, Coleraine

Bonfire

B onfire, bonfire, don't be slow, light up and tall you grow.
O il and petrol to help you burn and stop you from being slow
N othing to stop you burn in the dark of the night at the hill and park
F iery and orange colours light up the whole street to have a
laugh and a lark at the park.
I nteresting shadows scare the children away all safe and sound
in their house to get snuggled up and sleep.
R aging flames spurt to the sky in a rage at the stars that
twinkle and leap.
E very Hallowe'en the bonfire burns to the joy and excitement of all.

Ellie Mcilreavy (11)
Coleraine High School, Coleraine

The Grapefruit

I pick it up and feel its skin,
The orangey-yellow skin,
Its odourless, thick skin,
Its touch is so beautiful,
As beautiful as a spring morning.

As I compress its round body,
It feels firm, firm, firm.
But there's a little tenderness,
This is what I want
Nothing more, nothing less.

Its beautiful body is sliced,
And a fresh smell of summer rises.
The inside is a deep red
The juice dripping off it,
Soaks my fingers.

I take a bite
And its juice caresses my lips.
It's comforting me,
It's sending me to Heaven
I've never felt so alive.

Charlotte Kilgore (13)
Coleraine High School, Coleraine

Joy

Joy is a little girl wearing a pink flowery dress.
She is skipping through a field of flowers and singing softly.
Humming a merry tune, she makes a daisy chain.
Her cheeks are a soft, rosy-pink, just like her dress.
She scoops up a handful of colourful flowers but her mother is calling.
Joy hurries home to make her mum happy with a beautiful bunch
of buttercups.

Rebecca Millar (11)
Coleraine High School, Coleraine

Jubjub Bird

(Inspired by 'Jabberwocky' by Lewis Carroll)

The Jubjub bird is fierce and bad,
And sometimes I think you will find,
The jubjub bird can make people mad,
Because people can't read his mind.

He hunts around the wood,
Scaring little rats and mice,
Beware he's looking for food,
And he's wanting something nice.

In the evening time he rests,
He's worn out from the day,
Here he goes to make his nest,
He's asleep, now stay away.

Tamsin McKissick (13)
Coleraine High School, Coleraine

Hallowe'en Night

Jack-o'-lanterns with a bright glow,
Bats passing by, swooping quite low.

If you don't like Hallowe'en night,
Be prepared, you might get a fright.

If you're out to say trick or treat,
Be aware of the creatures, which you might meet.

Ghosts and goblins breaking the laws,
Wait to you see what trouble they've caused.

To go out, don't hurry,
For you might really worry.

Just sit tight,
On this scary night!

Jenna Rainey (11)
Coleraine High School, Coleraine

My Family!

My mum is called Jayne
She is the greatest
I love her to pieces
'Cause she is my mum.

My dad is called Sammy
He works real hard
He keeps me with the trend
And I drive him round the bend.

My bro is called Mark
He can be really annoying
But I really love him
'Cause he's my bro

My sis is called Tara
She's so cute
I love her dearly
And I know she loves me too.

We are a family
And we bond really good
We love each other
And that's all there is to it!

Chloé McConaghie (13)
Coleraine High School, Coleraine

Bonfire

B onfire Night is the best night ever
O il to light the bonfire forever
N ever let them blow you out
F lames so bright the children shout
I nside the bonfire ever so bright,
   different colours light up the night
R ed-hot flames that keep us warm
E veryone knows they could do us harm.

Amy McDowell (11)
Coleraine High School, Coleraine

An Acrostic Of Bonfire Night

B uild it up high, right up to the sky,
O n go the wooden chairs and old tables too.
N ow let's light it,
F izzle, fizzle, music to our ears,
 I s everbody enjoying themselves?
R ising up, the flames reach the old sofa at the top,
E veryone's cheeks are aglow.

N earby the fire brigade stand on edge.
 I watch them throw on wood and paper.
G uy Fawkes is thrown on the bonfire.
H ow exciting this is.
T he flames starts to die down and eventually go out.

Mollie Ferguson (11)
Coleraine High School, Coleraine

The Octopus

The little octopus that lives under the sea,
Looks rather strange, but nothing like me!
She is red, orange, yellow and blue,
She is normally called Octopus Sue.

She's friends with all the fish and the whales,
She also tells many a tale.
She is always happy joyful and fun,
Throughout the whole day until down goes the sun.

I do not see her as often as I wish,
But I know she gets company from all of the fish.
She always has a smile for me,
Every time I see her swimming under the sea.

Hazel Ramsey (12)
Coleraine High School, Coleraine

Hallowe'en

Hallowe'en is here
Children they should fear
On Hallowe'en night
Who knows what you will hear.

Children going trick or treating
All the sweets they will be eating.

Ghosts and ghouls, big black cats
Witches flying wearing hats
Pumpkins lit with scary faces
Where you see them all sorts of places
Eating nuts and shouting loud
In the streets what a crowd.

It only comes once a year so stay away and do not fear!

Danni Mullaghan (12)
Coleraine High School, Coleraine

Bonfire

A bonfire is like a lion,
With his beautiful golden mane.
He roars and he growls,
As he waits for his prey.

He hides in the bushes and branches,
As he waits for his lunch.
He'll eat anything you give him,
And that includes you!

This lion has eaten a few people,
Some you may know.
So next time you're near a bonfire,
Remember the lion is waiting for you.

Alice Eustace (11)
Coleraine High School, Coleraine

A Winter's Night

Walking up the road water squelching inside my shoes,
My feet slip over the icy pavement,
The wind is so strong my face is numb,
I see the lights of my house shining brightly.

I can see the next-door neighbours' television lights flashing,
I wish I was inside,
My coat is heavy now with the beating rain.

I reach my front door and open it wide,
I can smell my tea,
My mum comes to welcome me,
The hot chocolate warms my hands.

I think to myself,
How safe I am in here,
Warm and cosy,
I am safe in here, I am safe.

Aislinn Gregg (11)
Coleraine High School, Coleraine

A Stormy Night

The bucketing rain pours down,
Like an owl after its prey.
I hear my dog barking in the darkness,
As I search for him in the hail.

My foot squelched into an ankle deep puddle,
Suddenly a fork of lightning streaked through the sky.
My dog is running at full speed towards me,
And pushes me down to the cold mud.

Now I am safe and clean at home again,
Under my duvet I snuggle down to sleep.
I feel the heat of the open fire,
My dog rests against my feet.

Rachel Abernethy (11)
Coleraine High School, Coleraine

My Child

A beautiful silken body
Wrapped in silken thread,
Covered in sparkling dancing diamonds,
Embroided with crystals.
Majestically he stood
Beside his creation,
Proud and joy-filled,
His cause and true meaning in life
Spun together in flesh and blood,
Like a small sample of Heaven.

My child how I adore
Your tiny fingers and face,
Your soft, velvet skin,
Pink lips and beautiful shimmering blue eyes.
Every time I look at you
I think to myself,
What a lovely, lovely creation
I have made like a sample of Heaven.

Jordan Campbell (11)
Coleraine High School, Coleraine

Anger

Anger is a red ball of fire,
With black smoke billowing.
Anger is acid and sour like an unripe lemon,
Leaving a bitter taste in your mouth.
It's smoky and stuffy,
You find it hard to breathe.

Anger is a lion roaring,
Making the ground beneath tremble.
Anger is a thundering waterfall,
Crashing onto the rocks.
Anger flares up,
Destroying everything in its path.

Fiona Xiaofei Huang (11)
Coleraine High School, Coleraine

And She Was Gone

This girl she is so lost,
And she is so cold and lonely,
She wishes she could be free,
Like the snow and ice and frost.

She longs to be a bird,
She wants to fly away,
To fly to a foreign land,
To be free from poverty.

She wants to feel the warmth
Of a blazing hot house fire,
'I long to be in from this cold,
This is my one desire.'

One time this girl was crying
In the moonlight of the night,
This girl inside, felt she was dead
Because she missed her family and friends.

She thought back to that terrible day
When the blazing fire started,
She wished she could've gone with them
Away with them to Heaven.

She walked to a river
And sat at the river's bank,
She threw in a pebble,
She watched as it sank,
Then suddenly there was a light, bright and long,
She walked into it and she was gone.

Lauren Iris Andrews (11)
Coleraine High School, Coleraine

A Surprising Storm

We ran out of the beach so quickly,
I was so scared, I was so scared,
We saw the lightning lash across the sky,
We had to get home the long way.

I clenched Mummy's hand so tightly,
I was still scared, I was still scared,
We watched the warm cars go by,
We got so wet that day.

As soon as we got in,
Mummy got out warm towels,
I was so warm, I was so warm,
Then I had some tea.

I set the tea up against my chin,
My dog was so cold she howled,
I was still warm, I was still warm,
That was a stormy day for me.

Jeni Campbell (11)
Coleraine High School, Coleraine

Hallowe'en Night

Pumpkin faces and treacle pie
In the big moon-filled sky
The witches and vampires are about
With their broomsticks and cloaks wide open out
The guy is lying on the ground
Waiting patiently to be found
By the small and the tall
The long, dark night is beginning to fall
Be careful you don't get a fright
On this very spooky Hallowe'en fright night

The Hallowe'en night has been and gone
The sun's now rising, it's now dawn.

Laura Harper (12)
Coleraine High School, Coleraine

Bonfire Night

On Bonfire Night we all gather round
The dazzling, sparkling, bright coloured light
Children are running all around
Laughing and shouting with all their might

Hear the parents chatting
Of how the day has been
Letting the heat just drift them away
Into the stillness of this great night

There goes the fireworks, hear them so promptly
Lighting the sky like a big glitter ball
All different colours bright and sparkly
Smell all the smoke descending from the sky.

Lydia Storey (11)
Coleraine High School, Coleraine

Trick Or Treat

T omorrow will be Hallowe'en
R ows of costumes in shops are seen
I will be dressed up as an ugly old witch
C reeping, crawling and hiding in a ditch
K eeping quiet, trying not to be found

O r knocking on doors watching people frown
R ight and left each side of the street

T aking time to scare everyone we meet
R eady for fireworks - one, two, three, *boom!*
E ach exploding firework met with glee
A t the end of the night we all agree
T is the best Hallowe'en party there ever has been.

Rachel Wallace (11)
Coleraine High School, Coleraine

Weather's Nightmare

Out on the road
The lightning cracks down
Bitter cold air
Bites my poor fingers numb.

The cars on the road shake
With the rumble of thunder
My shoes squelch
With snow and rain.

Oh, how I wish to be home
Cuddled by the fire
When will it happen?
Will it ever?

Now I am home, safe but wet
I snuggle to sleep
I never want this nightmare
Ever again.

Shannon Dunlop (11)
Coleraine High School, Coleraine

Dark Winter Night

All alone on a dark winter night
Walking briskly home
The rain pours, the wind howls
And chills me to the bone.

All alone on a dark winter night
Walking home so fast
Something in the forest howls
Rain pours down the back of my neck.

All alone on a dark winter night
Bursting into the door
Kicking off my sodden boots
Home at last, safe and sound.

Hazel Clarke (12)
Coleraine High School, Coleraine

A Wet And Windy Day

Waiting for the bus
Rain beating down
And clashing off the ground
Wind blowing the leaves from the trees.

My fingers and my nose
Are as cold as ice
I wish I were at home
Beside the warm fire.

Bus comes at last
I climb on, it is warmer than outside
I arrive home to a warm cup of tea
I sit on a soft chair and sip my tea
Now I feel much better
Snuggled up at home.

Judith Johnston (12)
Coleraine High School, Coleraine

It's Raining, It's Pouring

The trees are all dripping
Blue drips of cold water
The clouds are all split out into the open
No sign of a bird, just rain and more water.

Puddles are getting large
And the lake is getting full
The clouds are getting darker
And I'm closer to home now, phew!

I'm at home at last
In my warm room
Getting ready for a warm bath
It's time to go to sleep now, night-night.

Alex McAlister (11)
Coleraine High School, Coleraine

Hallowe'en

It's Hallowe'en today,
So we have to get ready,
To be aware of all the frights tonight.

First we carve the pumpkin's face,
And set it outside our door.
And next on my list is my really scary costume,
Which I'm going to wear trick or treating tonight.
I see my friends in their costumes,
A witch, a clown and Dracula.
But of course my costume is the best,
For I am Frankenstein.
Once we have finished trick or treating,
We all go back to my house,
To split all our sweets equally.
There are lollies, toffee apples, chocolate apples and sweets,
And piles and piles of chocolates.

It's the end of the night,
Not too many frights,
And Hallowe'en is far from sight.

Sarah Dempster (11)
Coleraine High School, Coleraine

Winter

Winter is when the snowman comes out to play
Beckoning the children to enter his world of whiteness
In the gardens mountains of snowballs wait anxiously to be thrown
Holly leaves pierce the air, red berries brightening
Jack Frost's world of whiteness
Icicles, like sharp spear heads
Hang from snow covered walls

Our winter alarm clock wakes us each morning
Jack Frost is the alarm clock nipping us out of our beds
His sharp nails telling us winter has come.

Lauren McQuilken (11)
Coleraine High School, Coleraine

A Cold Night

I'm outside playing
With all of my friends,
I start to feel trickles of rain
All over my head.

The wind is beating
Against the houses,
I wish I was in my warm bed
Cuddling up in my blankets.

We're running home
To get some shelter,
I'm inside my house
Feeling much better.

I get my pyjamas on,
Got into bed,
Rest my eyes,
Then drift into sleep.

Rachel Minihan (11)
Coleraine High School, Coleraine

Storm

Walking down from the bus stop
The rain is beating off the ground
The wind is tossing me about the stony path
Cars go past and splash me.

I'm close to my house now
I can see the garden
Just two more minutes to go
And I'll be out of this storm.

I am at the front door now
I am surrounded by heat
I can smell the dinner cooking
I am so happy to be out of that storm.

Rachel McQuillan (11)
Coleraine High School, Coleraine

The Weather's In A Bad Mood

Rushing home from high school
Jack Frost's icy breath on my neck
The cold makes my head hurt
I want to get home.

The lightning is crackling above my head
Booming thunder is teasing the jagged lightning
Drip-drop the rain is starting
The beginning of a storm.

I speed along the icy path
Nearly slipping on some black ice
I reach the front door; I open it
And reveal my warm yellow hall.

I rush into the living room
My mum takes one look at me and says,
'I'll put the kettle on'
I sit and drink my tea on my safe leather sofa
I'm safe and warm at last.

Amy Macauley (12)
Coleraine High School, Coleraine

Waiting In Weather

Waiting for Dad to come and get me
The rain pelting so hard it hurts
Soaked to the skin in my uniform
Just wish he would hurry up.

My hands I can't feel them
They're so cold and numb
Shivering in silence watching the time
Just wish he would hurry up.

Finally I see his car
I get in, he has the heating on fully
It's so warm, it feels so good
I wish I never have to go through this *again!*

Louise Wilson (12)
Coleraine High School, Coleraine

Cold Snow

I am standing at the bus stop
It has been snowing.
I feel cold, my fingers are numb,
All I can hear are people's footsteps
Crunching in the cold, white snow.

My bus peers around the corner
It stops and I step inside,
To the lovely warm air
Then I sit down.

The bus drives down the road,
It comes to my house,
I step out to the cold once again,
Then run to the warmth of my house.

I enter my house,
And see a lovely log fire,
I snuggle down on the chair,
Then drift off to sleep.

Amy McIntyre (11)
Coleraine High School, Coleraine

Out On A Wet Day!

Out on a wet day riding my bike,
The grey clouds are blocking the sun's bright glow,
The wind is pulling back my hair,
The rain is soaking right through my clothes.

Pedalling hard to beat the wind,
My eyes start to water as it hits my face
My legs start to hurt, I feel I can't go anymore,
But look! I'm almost at my front door.

Opening the door then closing it behind me,
Leaving the wind out in the cold,
In the warm kitchen I hear my mum call me,
It seems I am home just in time for my tea.

Naomi Todd (11)
Coleraine High School, Coleraine

Bad Weather

Me and my mum are walking together taking my dog for a walk,
It's cold and wet, it's very bad weather,
My coat is zipped up tight together.

The wind and the rain are rushing together, blowing my hood down,
The wind and the rain are soaking me and my mother.
I wish I was home sitting with my brother in my warm, safe house,
There is no one about, just me and my mother.

The cars are rushing past fast and furiously,
Me and my mum are nearly home,
The wind is blowing our hoods down together,
The rain is making our hair all wet, we are soaking.

We walk on the driveway, at last we are home,
The house is lovely and warm,
The TV is buzzing with EastEnders.

I go up and get washed and put my pyjamas on,
I wrap a warm blanket around me,
I get in my bed, my mum tucks me in,
She slowly walks downstairs and I fall asleep.

Rebekah Quinn (11)
Coleraine High School, Coleraine

Winter Is Coming!

It's warm and toasty,
Fire light,
We drink hot chocolate,
Have a roast beef dinner,
Nice and warm.

It went silent,
We stood,
Looked out the window,
A chill went down my spine,
White and icy.

Winter is here again!

Victoria Logan (11)
Coleraine High School, Coleraine

Hallowe'en

The best time of year again is here,
A time for ghouls, fun and fear.
When ghosts, witches and vampires are on the prowl,
Can you hear the werewolves howl?

All the children decide what costume to wear,
A vampire, a ghost or a witch with long black hair.
They all think of the lollies, chocolate and sweets,
That they will get when they trick or treat.

Hallowe'en monsters are the scariest of all,
A vampire with fangs or Frankenstein standing tall.
There are witches, wizards and ghosts too,
Plus many more besides all waiting for you.

Then there are all the parties, which we have to attend,
Or if you're planning your own, all the invitations to send.
Then there are the fireworks, sparklers and Catherine wheels too,
They light up the sky with red, purple and blue.

But soon all the fun will come to an end,
Ghouls and ghosts are no longer our friends,
So now we shall all sleep safe and sound,
Until the next time Hallowe'en comes around.

Clare Cox (11)
Coleraine High School, Coleraine

Fallen Angel

I once stood at a cliff
Looking down below me
I saw a fallen angel
Her wings broken, never to fly again
Once beautiful now ugly
She had been robbed of her pride and joy
And as I stared at this girl
I realised that it was upon my own reflection
In the rain puddles that I looked.

Siona Morrow (13)
Coleraine High School, Coleraine

Autumn

Sunshine has gone,
Days draw in,
Nights are black as coal.

Leaves change colour,
Orange, brown and red,
Jack Frost reveals his power.

Farmers harvest crops,
Animals gather supplies,
Birds prepare to fly south.

Hallowe'en approaches fast,
Toffee apples, trick or treat?
Fireworks explode in the pitch-black sky.

Central heating on,
Wrap up warm,
Winter's only weeks away.

Hayley Elliott (12)
Coleraine High School, Coleraine

You Laugh, I Cry

You laughed when I cried,
You'd threaten then I'd hide.
You pulled my hair, mocked my laugh,
Tore my homework in to half.

You never left me alone,
Threatened me with a stone.
Every time I tried to ignore you,
You beat me up for that too.

Why ever did you bully me?
Why did you never see
That every time you pushed me aside,
Eventually led to my suicide?

Rachel Smyth (12)
Coleraine High School, Coleraine

Going Home

We're on our way home, it's 11 o'clock,
The wind is whistling like a hurricane eye,
Our car has broken down, we need to walk,
There's lightning as well,
It's like a light bulb blinking.

It's starting to snow,
I'm freezing cold and my fingers are numb.
There are trees falling down all over the place,
We're nearly home, not far to go.

We're home and I'm going to bed,
I'm nice and warm now.
I'm all cuddled up,
And it's bedtime now.

Night-night!

Elaine Simpson (11)
Coleraine High School, Coleraine

Flowers

Flowers are a beautiful thing,
Even fit for a righteous king.
Bringing colour into your home,
Looking pretty by the garden gnome.

Red and yellow and pink and blue,
Colours of the rainbow shining through.
Cheering our sadness, giving us glee,
Flowers are a reflection of you and me.

Flowers are a sign of happiness too,
Showing brightness and life in you.
For our special times or just for fun,
Flowers can say it for everyone.

Lauren Hunter (13)
Coleraine High School, Coleraine

The Runaway

All you can hear are my feet pounding on the ground,
My hair is white with the snow falling down,
I feel as if I'm caught in the coldness,
But I'm determined to get home, I'm full of courage and boldness.

There is candlelight ahead,
A sign of my soft, warm bed,
I need to get there quick, in a hurry,
Oh Mum, I'm so sorry.

I'm nearly there, just a few steps further,
Just need to turn this big, round corner,
I'm so scared, I need to get home,
Oh, how I wish I'd never gone.

Here I am, back, what a delight,
I made it to the candlelight,
I'm safe enclosed, and I have to say,
Oh, I'm so sorry I ran away.

Lily Rebekah Sittlington (11)
Coleraine High School, Coleraine

Autumn

The leaves fall off the trees,
Children kick them in the breeze,
Making them crunch beneath their feet,
It's cold outside, there is no heat.

Birds fly to warmer places,
They make new homes in these new places,
The birds have more food o eat,
And it's warmer, plenty of heat.

After autumn winter comes,
Now the cold, dark nights come.
Winter is cold which brings snow,
Now the children play in the snow.

Claire Wilson (13)
Coleraine High School, Coleraine

The Storm

I'm sitting at home
All cosy and snug,
Looking out of the window
Under my rug.

It's raining outside,
But that's OK,
At least I'm not
Going out to play.

Now there's a frightening gale
And rumbling thunder,
Lots of battering hail,
Will there be lightning I wonder?

Oh no! I'm scared,
The lights have gone out,
I don't think this storm
Will ever go out.

But I was wrong,
This frightening gale
And battering hail,
Have all disappeared,
I should not have feared.

Catherine Campbell (12)
Coleraine High School, Coleraine

First Snow

The first snow of winter falls
Snowmen everywhere dressed up like dolls
Snowball fights in the school ground
Then comes detention, shh! not a sound.

Sitting in English in the cold,
Wishing I had something hot to hold
Watching the snowflakes fall to the ground
Floating down without a sound.

Lisa Douglas (12)
Coleraine High School, Coleraine

Hallowe'en

Hallowe'en is my favourite time of year,
A fireworks display,
It's nearly here.

Fireworks crackling in the air,
Babies crying,
Mum's in despair.

Children at your door,
Looking for a treat,
Some say a phrase like, 'Smell my feet!'

Chocolate apples,
They're so yum,
Ducking for them is such fun.

Walking to school, spent fireworks on the ground,
Not long now to the jingle bell's sound.

Sarah Breen (12)
Coleraine High School, Coleraine

My Life

Up in the old willow tree on the very top branch, we sat.
My family and I have been here since early spring.
We have seen the beauty of the setting sun
And bathed in the morning dew.
Our Mother Willow has kept us safe from any harm.

The birds set up home among us
And lay their eggs to hatch.
Little boys on our branches climb.
Badgers, owls, insects in our mother hide,
Coming out when darkness falls.

But now the days are getting shorter,
And the nights are getting colder.
As we sway gently in the autumn breeze,
Just waiting for when we leave our old Mother Willow Tree.

Megan Ferguson (12)
Coleraine High School, Coleraine

Recipe For A Perfect Outfit

Begin with bags full of *style!*
This will make a mixture of colours.
Add a twinkle of glamour
For that extra bit of pop star.
Mix in a bag full of money,
Of course it'll be the best.
Next stir in a cute mini skirt,
A hat and a T-shirt at that!
Or there's the question,
What about shoes?
A nice pair of boots
Or sandals will do.
In order to make the perfect little number,
Bake for 20 minutes, no longer
And serve with a nice figure,
Not too thin and not too plump.

Samantha Greenhill (11)
Coleraine High School, Coleraine

Seasons

When leaves are falling all around,
with all the different colours,
you will know it's autumn.

When the ground is covered
with footprints all around,
you will know it's winter.

When you see many flowers growing
with lovely bright colours,
you will know it's spring.

When you see everyone running with buckets and spades,
all wearing shorts and T-shirts,
you will know it's summer.

Cathy Callaghan (13)
Coleraine High School, Coleraine

Changing Seasons

Spring brings tulips and daffodils,
Beautiful blooming trees,
Juicy grass growing all around,
Signs of new life everywhere.

Summer brings lots of warmer days,
Colour is all around,
Butterflies flit from flower to flower,
And bees go buzzing by.

Autumn brings red, gold and brown leaves,
Dancing in the wind,
Like little ballerinas,
Twirling faster, faster and faster.

Winter brings swirling snowflakes,
Like fairies in the air,
They fall onto the earth,
Like a soft, white quilt.

Erin Smith (11)
Coleraine High School, Coleraine

A Perfect Recipe

A Recipe For The Perfect Day

Begin with bags full of sunshine,
This will make a mixture of fun and pretty flowers,
Add a teaspoon of sweet smell,
And an ounce of grass.
Mix with lots of children having fun
For added fun.
Next stir in happy parents,
Or no teachers,
Bake for one hour
And serve with the love of your heart.

Lydia Morrell (11)
Coleraine High School, Coleraine

Up In The Sand Dunes

Sitting in a secretive place,
Watching the busy world.
Boats gently drifting,
On the sparkling ocean.

Looking below me,
People are as small as ants,
Some are simply strolling,
Children are building with sand.

Waves are crashing against the rocks,
Light winds are blowing.
Sand is going into my eyes,
The caves have an eerie echo.

The blazing sun is setting,
It's getting quite cold.
The tide is coming in,
So everyone is going home.

Chloe Holmes (12)
Coleraine High School, Coleraine

A Perfect Marriage

Begin with a bag full of love
Followed by a pinch of spice.
Next stir in some family and friends.
Add an ounce of happiness,
You could also add a bunch of trouble!
Add a bowl full of sweetness,
Cook in the oven for an hour
And serve with smiles and laughter.

Lynsey Purdy (11)
Coleraine High School, Coleraine

Blizzard

Out by the road
In front of my house,
The sky is layered
With dark forbidding clouds.

Snow swirls around me
Chilling my face,
Ice covers the ground,
Mist fills the space.

The air becomes frosty
Darkness prevails,
Fog blocks my view,
Snow hides the trails.

The houses are welcoming,
Their windows ablaze,
Smoke flows from their chimneys
As I take one last gaze.

I trudge into my house
And climb into bed,
I cuddle my dog
While thoughts buzz in my head.

Emily Mesev (12)
Coleraine High School, Coleraine

Recipe For A Perfect Mum

Begin with bags full of smiles,
This will make the mixture thick with laughter.
Add a teaspoon of kindness
And an ounce of friendliness.
Mix with enjoyment.
For added spice mix in sugar.
Next stir in generosity
In order to sparkle and shine.

Sarah McCreadie (11)
Coleraine High School, Coleraine

The Hunter

Shifty, golden eyes of a sunbeam coat
Glance across towards morning light,
Sliver knives of large wide paws,
Clasping through dusty earth.

Seeing a silhouette, the hunter hits the ground,
Stalking, eyes fixed on future lunch,
A jumpy, foolish, young antelope,
Grazing among long blades of gold.

Shoulders shifting, creeping quickly,
No sound rising from her paws,
Slowing, padding, pulls to a halt,
Crouching down, giving her war *roar.*

The antelope shrieks, quickly dances in panic,
Before the ambush hunter claws onto his back,
One last cry as he is dragged to the ground,
As the blade of death slices his throat.

The proud young hunter hauls her strangled prey,
To a shaded old tree in the heart of her plains,
Laying down by a rock, sliver knives clutching her meal,
The lioness smirks, prize freshly won.

Amy McConkey (12)
Coleraine High School, Coleraine

Recipe For A Perfect Outfit

Begin with bags full of stars,
This will make the mixture soft and cushion-like,
Add a teaspoon of sugar,
Add an ounce of honey,
Mix with cinnamon
For added spice.
Next stir in some icing.
Bake for 25 minutes
And serve with softness.

Hannah Rankin (11)
Coleraine High School, Coleraine

Ocean

Wetsuit is necessary
To keep out the cold!
Everybody loves it,
Young or old.
On your bodyboard,
You skim through the waves,
The ocean's refreshing spray
Cools down your burning face.
Below the surface,
Under the depths,
The creatures you can't see
Are getting swept up in nets
For the fishermen's tea.
The dolphins swimming
With elegance and beauty,
The sharks protecting their territory,
They feel it's their duty,
So these you see
Are the reasons why
I love the ocean and the creatures
Not visible to the eye.

Shauna Platt (12)
Coleraine High School, Coleraine

A Recipe For A Perfect Friend!

Begin with bags full of kindness,
Take a small amount of height,
Add a lovely attitude.
While stirring, add some looks,
Put in a pinch of strength,
Stir for 10 minutes then pour into a pink bowl.
To add some flavour, put in some style,
Serve with lots of friends,
And a perfect friend you have made.

Taylar Wilkinson (11)
Coleraine High School, Coleraine

Bad Dreams In Weather

In the cold, rainy day
I think about running,
Running home to the warmth,
But I can't, I'm at least a mile away,
I wouldn't be able to make it all in one go.

I start walking quicker,
The rain beating harder and harder.
It feels like stones getting thrown on top of me,
So hard I feel like my back is breaking,
But I keep on walking on.

When I get closer to my destination,
The rain beats down harder,
To try and hold me back,
But I push on and on.

I get at least twenty metres away when
I wake up.
I realise it was all a dream,
Thank goodness, I'm all cuddled up,
Under a big, thick, warm duvet.

Jordan McCahon (11)
Coleraine High School, Coleraine

Recipe For A Perfect Friend

First take bags full of kindness,
this will make the mixture sticky and oozing with perfectness.
Add a teaspoon of clothes and shopping.
Add an ounce of secrets.
Mix with a trustful of friendship
for added fun and enjoyment.
Next stir in sparkle and glitter
or giggles and laughs
in order to have a girly sleepover.
Bake for sunshine minutes.
Serve with cream.

Jessica Elliott (12)
Coleraine High School, Coleraine

Someone Else

I'm sitting in the sandhills,
Gazing at the sea.
Wishing that I could be
Someone else but me.
I always wonder silly things that could never happen,
It annoys me when I think about this even when I'm napping.
I feel awful when I think that I can't do anything,
And that everyone else is going around with all the new bling.
I then snap out of the daze with a lick on the face from my dog,
I run home before I get caught in the fog.
My mum comes home with a new phone for me,
I think to myself *could it possibly be?*
I could maybe be in the cool gang now,
To show off my phone I go out with my bow-wow!

Zoë McCook (12)
Coleraine High School, Coleraine

A Recipe For A Perfect Horse

Begin with bags full of love,
This will make the mixture of a lifetime.
Add a teaspoon of cheekiness
And an ounce of kindness.
Mix with joy
For added friendliness.

Next stir in big loving eyes
Or cheeky ones
In order to make her be nice.

Bake for 30 minutes and leave for two hours
And serve with the perfect owner.

Alannah Cardwell (11)
Coleraine High School, Coleraine

Unexpected Weather

I remember the day
That was bright and sunny,
I even felt like
A small white bunny.

I could feel a patter
On my head,
But then it began
To thump like lead.

It wasn't just raining
It began to lash,
Oh, how it made
The roads look a hash.

I started to dart
From shop to shop,
People started staring
While they watched me hop.

I was nearly home,
I could see my house,
So I started to run
Like a little mouse.

There I was
Without a care,
All curled up
With my teddy bear.

When my mum came
To give me a warm drink,
She found me sleeping
Within a blink.

Demi Nicolle Black (12)
Coleraine High School, Coleraine

The Badger

The owl makes her appearance,
Screeching piercingly.
The badger has awoken,
His nose brown and moist sniffing,
Constantly.
Slowly, silently he creeps,
Hoping to find his prey.
His ears prick up, he stops dead in his tracks.
He hears voices approaching,
Quickly, he scurries off to his safe home.

Confident of finding his prey,
Badger appears once more.
Eagerly he strides towards the forest.
Beneath his feet a little mouse scurries,
Leaves rustle in the breeze,
Birds sing sweetly in the trees.
Badger is disturbed,
His prey is lost.
Homeward bound he strolls,
Hungry and dejected.

Karen Adams (12)
Coleraine High School, Coleraine

Recipe For A Perfect Day

Begin with bags full of energy,
This will make the mixture fun.
Add a teaspoon of excitement,
And an ounce of happiness,
Mix with laughter
For added pleasure.
Next stir in a sprinkle of mischief
In order to enjoy the day.
Bake for one hour
And serve with care.

Issy Craig (11)
Coleraine High School, Coleraine

Neighbours

One of my neighbours is called Jill,
Ask her to do something and she will,
She loves wearing boardies,
And likes cotton wool,
I think my friend, Jill, is really cool.

Another of my neighbours is Rosie Brown,
She would never try and make me frown,
She loves Paul Frank
And likes rowing too,
And always hugs you when you're feeling blue.

Another of my neighbours is Becca Jane,
You could call her anything but plain,
She loves shopping with friends,
And is always nice to me,
Friends forever we will be.

Zara Leighton (12)
Coleraine High School, Coleraine

Recipe For A Perfect Day

Begin with bags full of fun,
This will make the mixture yum.
Add a teaspoon of laughter,
Add an ounce of money
Mixed with honey
For added pleasure.

Next stir in a little love,
Or a lot of fluff.
In order to make it nice,
Make it for three blind mice
And serve to your dear old
Mummy!

Rebecca McFaull (11)
Coleraine High School, Coleraine

The Man

Alone he sits
His only friends, the birds and trees
He comes every day to talk

It's cool today
So alone he sits rocking
Inside it is warm so there he sits
It's windy, the trees hit his window

He's scared
They are not his friends
He cries
But still they hit his window

It's warm today
Outside he goes fearing the unknown
But now it is peaceful and there he stays
Talking, laughing and so on.

Emma Jayne Bannister (13)
Coleraine High School, Coleraine

A Recipe For A Perfect Sister

Begin with bags full of fun,
this will make the mixture of sisterhood more lively.

Add a teaspoon of talent.

Add an ounce of funniness.

Mix with enjoyment.

Next stir in energetic or arty
in order to have lots of fun.

Bake with happiness

And serve with love.

Stacey Tosh (11)
Coleraine High School, Coleraine

Recipe For A Perfect Day

Begin with bags full of laughter
In order to make a smile.
Mix in a dose of family and friends,
This will make the mixture sweet.
Next stir in some sunrays of sunshine
To make the heart unseal.
Add a teaspoon of trust and love.
Meanwhile share a gossip
To catch up on everything.
Let all the feelings and emotions go
As you feel so happy to see everyone.
Bake for a day and the recipe will be complete,
So have some fun and giggles
And serve with cream
And the recipe will continue whenever you want.
As you have enjoyed the day so much,
It is everlasting love.

Karla-Jayne Stewart (11)
Coleraine High School, Coleraine

Recipe For A Perfect Dog

Begin with big brown eyes,
Take a small, wet nose,
Add long, silky ears,
Fold in some soft, smooth hair,
Mix in a dash of Blenheim,
A pinch of freckles,
Stretch out a long, waggy tail.
Add a pitter-patter of tiny paws,
Pat gently and leave to rest,
Handle with care,
Bake to perfection,
Turn out to play,
Serve with lots of hugs and affection.

Lynsey Adams (12)
Coleraine High School, Coleraine

A Recipe For The Perfect Parents

Begin with a bowl full of tender loving care,
Add a pinch of patience,
Drizzle in a dash of wisdom,
Mix together with a teaspoon of fun.

Next half a jug of holidays in the sun,
Mix in a pinch of all night parties,
Stir in a packet of barbecues by the sea,
Add a dash of happiness.

Stir together well with a pound of fun,
Add to the mixture a teaspoon of sense of humour,
Now mix with a jug of smiles,
Add a bag full of money.

Bake for thirty minutes in the sun,
Serve with a sprinkle of love,
A pound of hugs and a bowl of kisses,
I think my parents are perfect!

Gill Arbuthnot (12)
Coleraine High School, Coleraine

Recipe For A Perfect Friend

Begin with bags full of energy,
This will make the mixture bubbly.

Next a bowl of smiles,
A pinch of enthusiasm,
A dash of care.

Mix in laughter and fun with
A jug full of determination.

Serve with lots of love.

Ellen McKinney (12)
Coleraine High School, Coleraine

Night's Storm

I'm alone in the dark, the rain stings my face
While the wind howls like a million fierce wolves
I'm waiting, I'm cold, but no one's around
There's nowhere to go, the road just goes on.

I begin to feel a shadow approaching me
'Who's there?' I call out, but no one replies
I hurry myself, scared as a mouse being hunted as prey
I'm running, I'm running, but there's nowhere to run to.

Where do I go or do I give up?
This dark shadow appears again in front of me
It puts its dark hand on my shoulder, I shiver with fear
For who is beyond that dark, creepy shadow?

The shadow steps into the moonlight to reveal who it is
I can't believe my eyes! For beyond that dark shadow
It was my dad all along, he smiles at me and carries me home
At my front door stands my mum with blankets and tea.

I'm in my living room now with my mum and dad
Now I'm safe from all dangers, I start to feel my eyelids close
The end of my trouble-filled day.

Meryl Gamble (12)
Coleraine High School, Coleraine

Farming Life

Here comes the rain again, the straw is getting wet,
The old cow's lying in the field and I think she needs a vet.
My dog feels winter coming on, he's getting old, my friend,
And if he lives another year, he'll be getting near the end.
They're paying even less for milk and charging more for feed,
I've got to pay for this month's bills and buy some barley seed.
Oh roll on winter, bring back the sun
Cos a farmer's life is not much fun.

Thomas Kelso-Mason (12)
Coleraine Academical Institution, Coleraine

Teacher

As he thundered in, the floor creaked,
He opened his mouth and we all freaked.
He set us a pile of work to do,
And wouldn't let anyone out to the loo.

When bold John Brown didn't hand in his work,
The teacher snarled and went berserk.
We all trembled; he cast his eyes around,
They looked at me; I dropped to the ground.

Next he went purplish-red in the face,
And told us we were a 'flamin' disgrace'!
He gave us lines for the noise we were makin',
When we got them finished our wrists were breakin'.

When the bell rang, we sighed with relief -
He could not cause us any more grief.
But then he yelled, 'Boys, stop messin'!
Don't you know it's a double lesson!'

Andrew Cunning (12)
Coleraine Academical Institution, Coleraine

What Is A Great Mind?

What is a great mind?
Is it someone you believe in
Or is it someone who believes?
Is it the writer who writes the song,
Or the singer who sings it?
Is it the scientist who discovered medical cures
Or the doctor who administers them?
Is it the athlete with power of the mind
Or the person who trained him?
Is it our leaders and politicians
Or the brave soldiers who fight?
Great strength of mind is in us all,
It's those of us who use their power to the full
Who are the 'great minds'.

Dylan Frew (14)
Coleraine Academical Institution, Coleraine

The Shadow

A strange person seems to follow me all day,
He's similar in shape and size to me
But he's alarmingly grey.
I don't know where he hides
When the sun goes down,
But when I get up, he's always around.
I sometimes think he speaks to me,
But convince myself it's the wind.
He's always at my heels - I told him to go -
He just grinned.
I've seen other people being followed by grey men,
I'm surprised to see it doesn't really bother them
But my grey man really bothers me
Until he goes away,
I know too that he'll follow me
Around again next day.

David Harding (12)
Coleraine Academical Institution, Coleraine

Hannah

She is summer to me, beautiful, warm.
She is more precious to me than all the diamonds in the world.
She is never sad but always happy.
She is like a panda, warm and cuddly.
She is as funny as Mickey Mouse; always laughing and happy.
She is the sun to my heart, the joy in my life.
She is the engine that keeps me going in life.
Her tongue stays still but she speaks to me in her own way.
She is the engine that keeps me going in life.
She is my niece,
My precious,
My Hannah.

Simon Clarke (12)
Coleraine Academical Institution, Coleraine

When I Am Older

When I am older, who knows what I'll be,
where I will travel, who I will see.
My whole life is before me, the future unknown.
Perhaps I'll be famous, who knows, I might!

I may be a rapper like 50 Cent,
crowds of fans following me wherever I go,
or I may be a doctor, a wrestler, a vet,
who knows what I'll be, I don't know yet.

As I am young, I'll dream while I can,
someday soon I'll become a man
with a job, a family and work to be done,
there'll not be much time for having fun.

The future's before me, I'll not worry,
no need to rush, no need to hurry.
When I am older, who knows what I'll be.
No matter what happens, I'll still be me!

Calvin Thompson (11)
Coleraine Academical Institution, Coleraine

Waiting

Sitting in a room with lots of other 'victims',
Staring at the dreaded door,
The one thing that I will have to enter,
Listening to nervous whispers all around,
People chewing, crying, sniffing, staring.
My hands are starting to sweat,
My head is spinning,
My toes are tapping in exasperation,
Then suddenly out of the blue
The man I'm dreading says,
'Next please. It's you!'

Philip Gilliland (12)
Coleraine Academical Institution, Coleraine

Great Minds

In this tiny world of ours, there're some momentous people,
Like Kelly Holmes, Elvis and Albert Einstein too.
But yet we all forget about the disabled and the feeble,
When really they're the heroes for everything they do.

Now you may wonder why someone who cannot walk a metre
Is more amazing than the athlete who can run a hundred miles.
Because underneath that misleading shell there is a great defeater
Of everything he has to do to survive, to make his life worthwhile.

It takes an extremely tenacious mind to bother going on,
When your life is like a pendulum, swinging out of control.
Yet these very resolute souls persist in staying strong,
And getting through tomorrow is their one and only goal.

So maybe now you understand that no matter how we try,
We could never go through what they must, and that I emphasise.
So now you can go home tonight and tell your family why
The great minds of our universe are hidden in disguise.

Gavin Kane (13)
Coleraine Academical Institution, Coleraine

I Lie In Fields Of Roses

I lie in fields of roses
With a river by the ferns,
A blazing sun up in the sky
When summer is just passing by.

I lie in fields of roses
With birds up in the sky,
I feel the wind upon my face
When summer's finished in this race.

I lie in fields of roses
With deer grazing in the sun,
Up in the sky the clouds are high
And summer seems to wave goodbye.

I lie in fields of roses
And watch the birds soar overhead,
As night now closes ever near,
Summer seems to disappear.

Jordan Millican (12)
Coleraine Academical Institution, Coleraine

Great Minds

There are two kinds of minds,
There are great minds like Albert Einstein
Then there is David Beckham's mind.

David may not know about relativity
But did Albert know how to bend a ball round the wall?
Is physics more important than football?

But what is the real meaning of great minds?
Does it mean you have an IQ of over 140
Or does it mean you have common sense?

Do other animals have great minds?
Could a bird be smarter than you
Or are humans the smartest?

Is brainpower in the mind
Or does it measure intelligence
Or do we really mind?

Do friends who think alike have great minds
As great minds think alike?
But fools seldom differ.

David McCluskey (11)
Coleraine Academical Institution, Coleraine

Maurice Green

The Olympics loom and not too soon,
Much atmosphere under the Athens' moon,
The crowd is buzzing, the athletes are jumping,
They're ready and waiting, adrenaline pumping.

Starter's orders, he's on the block,
Mind set on beating the clock,
The starter pistol delivers the shot,
That will take him through to the number one slot.

Running hard, hogging the ground,
How fast can his feet pound?
Heart beating, seconds fleeting,
Across the line, legs now screeching.

Pricked up ears,
Listening for cheers,
View the screen,
What's the scene?

One, two or three, what's the fate?
But today there will be no gold plate,
Four years on, that's the wait,
For another chance to be world great.

Ben Macaulay (11)
Coleraine Academical Institution, Coleraine

The Knight

Swords clashed,
Heads mashed,
Heroes lived and died.
Fires burned,
Stomachs turned
As men were burned alive.

Women screamed,
Swords cleaned,
Begin another day.
Slaughter more,
Cultures torn,
Keeping them at bay.

Cultivate,
Then migrate,
Start it all again.
Don't forget,
You will regret
You killed your fellow men.

So grab your sword,
There is reward,
And all your neighbours bring.
It is quite gory,
But there's glory,
Do it for your king!

Matthew Adams (13)
Coleraine Academical Institution, Coleraine

Simple Minds

Bag searching,
Pencil case rumbling,
Page number looking,
Pens scratching,
Line ruling,
Eyes wandering,
Hands covering,
Teacher glaring,
Ink still running,
Clock watching.

Daydreaming,
Teacher talking,
No one listening,
Paper pellets flying,
Teacher still grumbling,
Sun shining,
Where's the bell?
Period nearly over,
Break time - 15 minutes -
And here we go again!

Scott Lorimer (11)
Coleraine Academical Institution, Coleraine

Escape From Battersea

Red the lurcher was put in a home
Because his owners left him all alone.
The staff looking after him did their best
But Red was different from all the rest.

He watched the warden come and go
Because this old dog was not so slow.
At night when all was still and quiet
His tricks and ploys, they caused a riot.

He mastered how to open his lock
Then let out his friends to run amok,
They went into the kitchen and stole some food,
This dog was a very clever dude!

When the staff found the canines running free,
They asked themselves, 'How could this be?'
Video cameras were set, out of reach of paw,
Next day they couldn't believe what they saw.

Now Red has new locks on his door,
Will he be able to open them like before?
And as the warden closes his gate,
Red is planning his next escape . . .

Niall Adams (12)
Coleraine Academical Institution, Coleraine

Great Minds

Winston Churchill - man with a cigar,
Two fingers for victory - Britain went far,
He rallied the troops in the Second World War.
Germany defeated, Britain on top,
Only then could the fighting stop.

Adolf Hitler - looked like a rat,
Thought he could win the war.
Well, Britain saw to that!
Defeated and blue,
Took his life - well what else could he do?

Saddam Hussein thought he was clever,
With his threats to Britain - well I never,
Violence and terrorism going on forever.
Bush and Blair then saw to that mole
And found him cowering in his underground hole.

Then there's Bin Laden who thinks he's smart,
Murder and killing - well, where's his heart?
For al his wisdom - he'll soon go the same way
As Hitler, Hussein - and others who try
To abuse their power and cause others to die.

Great minds - we all think the same,
But to control through fear that's no game.
To use our knowledge to help each other,
Brother, sister, friend and mother,
If we all do some good - great minds - you and me.

William Doherty (14)
Coleraine Academical Institution, Coleraine

The Conker King

I was in the woods,
Walking I'd been
When I trod on something -
A bright conker I'd seen.

It still had its coat,
Its hard outer shell,
It looked quite battered -
A long story to tell.

I brought it to school
To show everyone,
I've started a great craze -
The battle's begun!

String wrapped round fingers
So tight they go blue.
If your conker splits,
You're in a bit of a stew.

My conker's a football,
As round as the sun,
As hard as concrete -
I've never not won!

The final is here
And I'm in it!
I take a hard swing -
His conker splits . . .

Across the playground,
I hear people sing,
'Three cheers for that guy -
He's the conker king!'

Glenn Elliott (12)
Coleraine Academical Institution, Coleraine

The Girl Next Door

One day at my granny's
A new girl moved next door.
The moment that I saw her,
My heart began to soar.

I finally found the courage
To ask her on a date.
But then I somehow lost it
And thought that I should wait.

I sent her cards and roses,
But didn't leave a name,
I sent her chocolate cookies
And found she liked them plain!

I found her name was Stacy,
She soon became my friend,
And then something happened
That I just had to mend.

We talked about movies and music,
She said I had a great mind,
I asked her if she liked me,
She said, 'Maybe' - love is blind.

Even though I'd asked her out,
We still are really good mates,
But now she has moved away,
I bleed as my heart breaks.

I cried and cried in sorrow,
It went on for weeks,
And I would have given anything
Just to hear her speak.

Now a new girl lives next door -
She thinks I'm really great,
Now I can't wait to ask her
To go with me on a date.

Callum McAfee (14)
Coleraine Academical Institution, Coleraine

Great Minds

'Great minds think alike'
That's how the saying goes,
Let's take time to remember
The ones that everyone knows.

Great mind, number one,
Is Einstein, oh what fun!
He wasn't so good in school, this one,
But he went on to prove the teachers wrong
By saying something no one had ever heard,
That was $E=MC^2$.

Great mind number two,
Is Newton - 'twas gravity he slew.
When the apple fell, it rang a bell.
A discovery had been made.
Now we know why things don't fly.

Great mind number three
Is Shakespeare you see.
Why did the bard
Make English so hard?
Did he know when he wrote
That we would still quote
'To be or not to be'?

Great mind number four -
Some water did pour
All over the floor
When, 'Eureka!' he shouted,
As the dress code he flouted.
Archimedes can still make us laugh.

'Fools seldom differ,'
That's how the saying ends.
Take a look around your class -
Any great minds amongst your friends?

Michael Wallace (13)
Coleraine Academical Institution, Coleraine

Great Minds Everywhere

Great minds are everywhere, spread wide and far,
From artists and poets to the makers of chew bars,
From long in the past or just today,
The list is nearly endless, let's just say.

Caesar, great leader of the mighty Roman Empire
Had huge tactical knowledge and eagle eye of a cricket umpire,
Hannibal Barker of Carthage who dared defy Rome,
Defeated, but fought on with rebels until he poisoned himself as
Roman troops descended on his home.

Archimedes, mathematician, inventor of formulae and the clever
Archimedes screw,
Cut down by a simple sweep of a Roman sword as trouble began
to brew,
Bill Gates of Microsoft and Windows, by far the most widely used
computer system,
Lennox Lewis, the boxing great really knows how to hit 'em.

The Conqueror, William of ten sixty-six
Went through Harold and the Saxons like a chainsaw through sticks.
The Lionheart, Richard, led the Fourth Crusade on his own,
After years of campaigning, from Muslim control did not shift the great
walled city of stone.

Hitler, evil leader of the mad Nazi Third Reich,
Invaded some countries and started a fight,
Slaughtered thousands of Jews and dropped tonnes of bombs,
Yet still you wonder why neo-Nazi racist parties live on.

Churchill who fought the Nazis and won,
Some help from other allies soon had them on the run,
Cigar in his mouth and smile on his face,
'V' symbol for victory and equality for every race.

Great minds are used for good and evil the same,
Destructive weapons roll from factories like dice in a game,
Though great minds die and fade away,
Truly great minds leave a long legacy,
There are many great things that you can still do,
Could the next great mind emerge as *you*?

Tom He (13)
Coleraine Academical Institution, Coleraine

I Lost My Shadow

I lost my shadow
One Saturday night.
I looked in my bedroom,
He was nowhere in sight.

I woke in the morning
To look for my friend,
I checked every cupboard
And round every bend.

Out of the front door
And into the sun -
Where was he hiding?
Where had he run?

But wait just a moment -
Who's that, dark and tall?
I glanced to my side -
There he was on the wall.

Terry Daly (12)
Coleraine Academical Institution, Coleraine

Pixie

She's small,
She's hairy,
She's vicious,
She's scary.
She has ears like a bat,
She has teeth like a rat.
She'll growl and she'll bite,
She'll howl at the night.
She stands six inches off the ground,
She's my mother's pet hound -
She's a Chihuahua.

Matthew Stavri (11)
Coleraine Academical Institution, Coleraine

Great Minds

My dad's great mind can . . .
     fix furniture,
     mend machines,
     tune tellies,
     plumb pipes
  and sort me out!

My grandad's great mind is made of memories . . .
     the man on the moon,
     the Second World War,
     the Queen's Coronation,
  and other stories for me.

My mum's great mind can do . . .
     horrible housework,
     clever cooking,
     terrible typing,
     dangerous driving,
     silly shopping,
     help with homework
  and all for me.

Stephen Best (11)
Coleraine Academical Institution, Coleraine

Great Minds

G is for great minds, there have been many,
R is for restless, these people are always looking to climb,
E is for exact, an inch out won't do,
A is for academic, there's hope for me and you.
T is for time and effort, a quick rush, never accepted,

M is for magic, never knowing what'll happen next,
 I is for intelligent, only the best will get through,
N is for nice and kind-hearted, these people know best,
D is for descend, no slope will do,
S is for smart, these people know all!

Nicolas O'Neill (13)
Coleraine Academical Institution, Coleraine

The Black Dragon

T he black dragon -
H atred in the air
E yes of dark blue.

B lack scales flowing all down its skin,
L egs are strong and sturdy,
A cid as its breath weapon,
C reatures flee from it,
K indness it's never heard of.

D aring heroes try to slay it,
R astlin the wizard enters the cave.
A nguish now creeps into his body;
G iven power comes to mind.
O range light flashes and the fireball explodes,
N ow the dragon is no longer a threat!

Ben Martin (13)
Coleraine Academical Institution, Coleraine

Autumn

H ealthy fruit ready to eat,
A pples to pick off the trees,
R ipe are the pears, ready to eat,
V ery busy farmers on the combines
E at all the food,
S horter days now,
T ractors ploughing the land.

Tomas Murray (16)
Kilronan School (Special SLD), Magherafelt

Autumn

A utumn is the best season of them all,
U nder the trees the leaves fall,
T he cooks bake the apple pie,
U nder the chestnut tree conkers lie,
M any farmers dig and sow,
N ow they can make things grow.

Steven McKeever (16)
Kilronan School (Special SLD), Magherafelt

My Home

I live in a bungalow
I have a bedroom that's blue
And from my window
There is a lovely view.
I see lots of houses
Tall trees and best of all
Very next door to me
There is a goldfish pond.

Sasha Bingham (11)
Lisanally Special School, Armagh

Banow

Banow is the name of my Auntie Sheila's dog,
He is big, brown and beautiful,
Soft and cuddly like a furry cushion,
He sees me and he licks my face.
He wags his tail and jumps about.
I say, 'Paw up,' and then, 'sit down.'
Banow does what I tell him
Because he's my friend.

Sheena McKenna (15)
Lisanally Special School, Armagh

Mr Snowman

I built a little snowman one year
When I was young in a cold icy world.
It was lots of fun,
It had a carrot for its nose
But it hadn't any toes.
It had coal for its eyes
And a bright scarf that ties.
All night we played in the bright moonlight.
Morning came and I had such a fright,
The sun came out and had such a fright,
The sun came out and spoiled our fun.
My little snowman was destroyed by the sun.

Philip Patton (13)
Lisanally Special School, Armagh

Clocks

Tick-tock, tick-tock,
I listen carefully to the clock.
It's like the sound
Of a dripping tap.
Big clocks, small clocks.
Round clocks, square clocks
All telling the time.
Time to get up,
Time to eat,
Time to speak,
Time to sleep.

Sandie Gibb (14)
Lisanally Special School, Armagh

I Love Food

I love food
It's so yummy and good
It fills my tummy
I eat too much says my mummy.
I like everything from spuds to cheese,
So please give me food, please, please, please.

I want some rabbit stew but my sister won't give me her bunny
So I'll have to settle for ice cream and honey.
Apple tart with sugar is oh so sweet
Strawberries and cream is another treat
Chocolate fudge sundae is for a fun day
But I could eat it every day except on a Monday.

Apples and oranges and bananas too
I also like my curry and vindaloo
Quiche and banoffee, I love them, I do
If I eat too much I'll need the loo.
All of this eating will have to stop
'Cause if I don't, my trousers will pop.

Adam Davison (11)
Magherafelt High School, Magherafelt

Mitsubishi EVO 8

The engine is like a roaring lion
The flames from the exhaust are as hot as lava
The wheels spin leaving clouds of smoke.
It's modified from the roof to the wheels.
It's as fast as a rocket.
It shines like silver,
The music vibrates like an earthquake
The neon's are as bright as the sun.
The tinted windows are as black as a pot
It's as powerful as an ox.

William Davison (13)
Magherafelt High School, Magherafelt

Christmas

Evening time is fading and it's getting dark
Cold winds are blowing
People are wrapped in jumpers, coats and hats.
What else can be expected as Christmas draws near?
Shopping for cards to write and post,
To wish everyone a merry Christmas.
Buying presents for family and friends.

Looking out the window, snowflakes begin to fall,
Can't wait until morning to snowball.
Building a snowman, oh what fun,
Carrot for a nose and coal for the eyes,
Every house with Christmas trees,
Flashing lights around windows and doors,
Just a few days left on Advent calendars.

Christmas Eve and families gather together
Choruses from the carol singers on the front doorstep
Everyone stands and listens
Presents piled under the Christmas tree
Ready to be opened.
Dinner being prepared in the kitchen
It's the night when you simply can't sleep.

Helen Hawthorne (12)
Magherafelt High School, Magherafelt

What Would I Do?

What would I do if I had no parents?
Sell the washing machine for a widescreen TV!

Shoot golf balls through the windows?
Put the car in Auto Trader and use
The money for PlayStation games.

Trade the bath for a swimming pool?
Sell the stairs for a fireman's pole
And make the garage into an Arcade.

Jordan Scott (12)
Magherafelt High School, Magherafelt

War

Artillery thumping,
Men screaming,
Wounded moaning,
Generals cursing,
As other man falls,
Jets zooming,
Bombs exploding,
Napalm burning,
Machine guns chattering,
Clay mores vaporising,
Booby traps killing,
Bullets cracking and whining,
Fires burning,
Men dying,
Interrogators torturing,
Tanks crushing,
Vietcong's attacking,
Sergeants ordering,
Helicopters landing all around,
Vietnam's bloody war!

Kyle Austin (12)
Magherafelt High School, Magherafelt

Hallowe'en

On Hallowe'en night I get a pumpkin and place a candle inside.
Outside I imagine I see ghosts and witches.
I see fireworks going off and rockets roaring into the sky.
My friends and I go trick and treating round the houses
But first we must put on our scary faces.
Children scream and rush into their houses scared by the sight of us,
Bonfires piled high are set alight.
They crackle and bang as the flames begin to leap into the night sky.
Parents and children gather round, holding sparklers.
Everyone is having so much fun on Hallowe'en night.

Stephanie Bruce (12)
Magherafelt High School, Magherafelt

Christmas

Christmas is here and it's Christmas Eve,
Oh, how exciting it is!
Looking at the Christmas tree and decorations,
Can't wait until tomorrow morning,
Santa will be coming tonight, so leave out some food.

The next morning has come,
Run up to the Christmas tree and
Oh, look at all the presents all over the floor!
It's so exciting.
Santa came last night but all he left was the crumbs,
He's so kind to us! Thanks Santa!

Once we had opened our presents,
We played with them.
But before we knew it, dinner was ready.
Christmas dinner was really nice,
So after, we watched Christmas movies.

Christmas is nearly over,
Christmas night we went to a party with all our family.
We played games at the party
But at the end of the day -
What is Christmas really about?

Laura Anderson (12)
Magherafelt High School, Magherafelt

Football

Football is my favourite game
I like to play it a lot.
But sometimes I end up
lying on the grass.

My favourite team is Man United
I think they are the best.
And when they have won the World Cup,
they are simply the best.

Matthew Campbell (11)
Magherafelt High School, Magherafelt

Autumn

The leaves swish round my back garden,
Swish, swish, swish, swish!
I tramp through the leaves in my back garden,
Crackle, crunch, crackle, crunch!
My mum brushes the leaves up,
Brush, brush, brush!
My dad burns the leaves,
Crackle, spit, crackle, spit!
The wind roars at night,
Roar, roar, roar, roar!
In the morning, the leaves swish round my back garden
once more,
Swish, swish, swish!
Mum and Dad look out of the window,
No, no, no!
The door bangs! Someone is at the door.
Bang, bang, bang!
The fireworks fly through the sky,
Zoom, bang, zoom, bang!
It's late at night, everyone goes to sleep.
Snore, snore, snore!

Timothy Sloan (12)
Magherafelt High School, Magherafelt

Hallowe'en

Hallowe'en is a spooky time when zombies,
Mummies and vampires are thirsty for blood
Always trying to scare people
Everybody goes round trick or treating
Looking for something good to eat.
There are always spooky castles,
Coffins and spooky decorations,
And getting Hallowe'en cakes.
Letting off fireworks and decorations,
Which we decorate the house with.

Karl Mitchell (11)
Magherafelt High School, Magherafelt

Hallowe'en

Hallowe'en
Very spooky
Lollies and sweets
All flavours and fruity.

Witches and ghosts
Very scary
Frightening letters in the post
Fake blood made from a red berry.

Hear a scream
From the top of the hill
Then you see that gleam
Now he is ready to kill.

Ghost stories
And horror films
Now you think of spooks worries
Ghouls, ghosts, goblins and evil spirits
Come out to shock you like a current.

Vanessa Mitchell (11)
Magherafelt High School, Magherafelt

Hallowe'en

Knock, knock on the door,
Trick or treat? Smell my feet.
Ghosts in the air, bat in the trees,
Children having fun on a gloomy night.
Sweets on the stairway, paper on the ground.
Fireworks banging, rainbows in the air,
Parties in the streets, kids all dressed up
Having fun ducking for apples.
Playing hide-and-seek. Peekaboo, I see you!
Others hiding in a cupboard with mice and
Loads of things that just ain't nice.

Nicola Purvis (13)
Magherafelt High School, Magherafelt

The Boy Who Had A Weird Dream

My desk's at the back of the class
Beside this real good-looking lass
When the teacher sees me talking
She makes me do some walking
And to the head's office I go.

On my way down
I put on my crown
And I say I'm the best in the class
But when I see him
I say to myself
I'd better start making amend.

When I go into the room
All I see is flowers ready to bloom
And then I remember
That this is December
And it's all one big dream.

Judith Hutchinson (12)
Magherafelt High School, Magherafelt

What Happens On Hallowe'en Night?

I looked out the window on Hallowe'en night
When I saw a witch outside. What a fright!
There were ghosts and ghouls all standing around
The bonfire outside, when I heard a sound.
I looked on the other side of town and
There was loud music and a lot of clowns.

Then I heard a strange knock at the door,
And I thought, *I can't live here anymore!*
I opened the door and there were people in wigs,
They were holding a bag which was very big.
Once they went away, I went back inside
And went to my room and looked outside.

Megan McKee (12)
Magherafelt High School, Magherafelt

Aliens

Aliens in spaceships, zooming here and there
Spinning around and up and down, in the Milky Way,
They're small and mean, with a hint of green,
They have a pair of eyes like two snot pies
And runny noses like firemens' hoses.

He turned around, I made a dash to get away,
I ran through every door in sight.
I ran, I ran with all my might,
Suddenly zap! Then all I could see was
Stars so bright.

He zapped me with his ray gun,
I found myself whizzing, whirling back to Earth,
I've woken up. Woo what a dream!
I wonder what tomorrow will bring?

Dean Steele (11)
Magherafelt High School, Magherafelt

School Holidays

Everyone can't wait
Until the school holidays are here
They all sit patiently
Watching the time draw near
Listening for the last bell to ring
Everybody cheers as off we go
Up the town to celebrate
We're off at last
Going home to lie and vegetate
Curled up the next morning
Cosy and warm in bed
Better than wait at the bus stop
For another school day.

Andrew Glendinning (12)
Magherafelt High School, Magherafelt

Skater's Heaven

Half pipe
Quarter pipe,
Grinding bar,
And a bowl.

Nose grind,
Board slide,
Tail grind,
And 50-50.

Ollie in
Kickflip out,
Up the slope
And jump the stairs.

Heelflip the kickers,
Hippy jump the benches,
Stalefish on the pipe
And end with a manual.

Ryan Duncan (12)
Magherafelt High School, Magherafelt

Hallowe'en

Hallowe'en will soon be here,
When the ghosts will appear,
Mums and Dads get off to work,
So they light some fireworks.

When the children go off to school,
They all act like a fool,
But they're only trying to act cool.

On Hallowe'en night
The children are all in sight
Running around the streets
To get some treats.

Jordan Yorke (11)
Magherafelt High School, Magherafelt

A Nature Walk

I walk along the grass,
moving across the ground.
I look up at the sky
And see what's around.

I look at the bare old trees,
Without any leaves.
I look down at the ground
And what do I see?
A bunch of leaves scuttering around.

I look at the grass,
Which is white with
The fog and see little
Tiny flowers with heads fallen off.

I look at the vegetable patch
And look to see
How my potatoes are getting on for
Harvest and my tea.

I check around and
Pick two or three,
Little flowers with
Tiny leaves.
I open the door
And walk inside,
Clean my feet and close the door.

Barbara Parke (11)
Magherafelt High School, Magherafelt

Family

F amily are the people you turn to when you're sad,
A lways there to help with an outstretched hand,
M any good times they give to you each and every day,
I t's marvellous to have a family who are great in every way,
L ove, protection, caring, it's available night and day,
Y ou really are a lucky person if your family is just like mine!

Katherine Currie (11)
Magherafelt High School, Magherafelt

On Hallowe'en

One Hallowe'en night,
I got a great fright,
I saw a ghost,
Or two, at the most.

I knocked on the door,
I heard a man roar,
He gave me some treats,
A small bag of sweets.

I saw a boy dressed up,
He had on a fake cut,
There were skeletons too,
And broomsticks that flew.

Witches and cats everywhere,
Bats and ghosts, what a scare!
Spooky sounds in the night,
Spiders and bats, what a fright.

Fireworks light the sky,
Going up really high,
Flying up for a while,
They must go up for a mile.

Leigh Gibson (12)
Magherafelt High School, Magherafelt

My Best Friend

F riends are forever
R unning after you
I f I had any problems
E ven any news
N o one could ever beat my
D elightful, hardworking, best friend in the world.

Rebecca Evans (11)
Magherafelt High School, Magherafelt

Winter

I like the snow,
Even if there is a chilly blow.
I'm freezing, I know,
But I still like the snow!

Ice-skating, the best,
But I need a rest.
Argh! A snowball, my brother is a pest,
He needs a psycho test!

Icy ground
I've found.
Children screaming and shouting, what a bad sound!
I don't go inside, I've made it abound.

Winter is a special time of the year,
The children throw snowballs in fear.
Sadly at the end of the year,
The snow will disappear!

Tanya Selfridge (12)
Magherafelt High School, Magherafelt

My Dog

Two summers ago I got a shock,
My parents had quite forgot
That of dogs, I was afraid,
Why had they bought one? I was dismayed!

He was fluffy and very small,
He had four brown patches in all.
He was active and hard to catch
We very quickly named him Patch.

Two years on, I wouldn't change him at all,
Even though he chases my ball.
My poem surely has a happy end,
As Patch has become my very best friend.

Rachel Michael (11)
Magherafelt High School, Magherafelt

Seasons!

Baby lambs are born in spring,
As you hear the birds sing,
The daffodils begin to bloom,
As we spring clean with our broom!

Summer is meant to be hot,
But mostly it's obviously not,
It's a time when we have fun,
Playing around in the sun!

Autumn starts to get cold,
As the flowers grow old,
Harvest time has come,
As the rain has begun.

As winter is near, we know
We are sure of the snow,
Outside it's cold to go!

Elaine Wilson (12)
Magherafelt High School, Magherafelt

My Idol

There he goes down the line
He's got the ball, isn't he fine?
All dressed in red from head to toe,
He's got the ball, as white as snow.

There he stands tall and strong,
Once you see him he can do no wrong,
There's pictures and posters of the team,
Watch this man, he's full of steam.

His name you'll want to know,
His autograph many are proud to show.
Wayne Rooney is his name
He's the man who will win the game.

Andrew Moore (11)
Magherafelt High School, Magherafelt

A Close Call

She crouches flat, so very flat
Beside the garden wall
She's quite still
So very still
There's no sound at all.

He flies down low, so very low
Just near the garden wall
He spies some food
Some lovely food
He thinks he'll have it all.

Then I scream, I really scream,
'Stay off the garden wall!'
The bird flies high
The cat moves on
Phew . . . that was a close call!

Richard Brown (13)
Magherafelt High School, Magherafelt

I Think My House Is Haunted

I think my house is haunted,
I hear creeks that go bump in the night,
And I get a big fright.

I think my house is haunted,
I hate it when night comes,
It's so scary, I just call for my mum.

I think my house is haunted,
I am glad the night is nearly over,
It's coming to dawn,
I start to yawn and morning finally comes.

Andrea Watson (12)
Magherafelt High School, Magherafelt

Shopping

Shopping is so great
When you take a mate
Down the town
So please do not frown
'Cause shopping is so great.

Earrings, jewellery and many other things,
Pretty gold rings,
Pearl white necklaces,
That come from space
And more wonderful things.

Everyone knows that shopping's the best
So have a guess
What's going to happen
In the future.

Rachel Bolton (11)
Magherafelt High School, Magherafelt

The Worst Thing About Football

Football is fun
It keeps you very fit,
But the worst thing is
The colour of the kit!

It's yellow with black stripes
And thick woolly socks,
When we run on the pitch
The other team mocks.

Even though they mock
We try to be so kind
Because they have forgotten
That they are three goals behind.

Nicky Brown (12)
Magherafelt High School, Magherafelt

Hallowe'en Times

At Hallowe'en time, people celebrate,
By dressing up and scaring people.
Everybody, trick or treats and gets lots of sweets,
The costumes are so scary and fierce,
That they even scare me a lot.

Everybody lights fireworks and they
Are very noisy, but lovely.
We throw things on the bonfire,
And the ashes fly freely in the sky.
I love Hallowe'en at night it is noisy.

Spiders, witches, ghosts, cats and bats
Are all the spooky things in a house,
On Hallowe'en parties.
Scary, spooky spiders and they're real spiders.
What's next, werewolves?
Faces peering out at you - me, anyone!
I don't think so!
That's Hallowe'en for you and me
Scary isn't it? Woooooh!

Evena Anderson (11)
Magherafelt High School, Magherafelt

A Mother's Love

My mother is so special
In many different ways
She treats me like a friend and son
Each and every day.
We do a lot of things together
No matter what's the weather
I always make her a cup of tea
To show her how much I care
I love my mum with all my heart
Each and every day.

Steven Stewart (11)
Magherafelt High School, Magherafelt

Lucky

She is soft and grey
She often wants to play
I get out her wee mouse
With which she plays around the house.

She wakens me in the morning,
I think she's giving me a warning,
To get out of bed and feed her
Or in my ear she will purr.

I really love my cat
I often give her a pat
Even when she's a bit mucky
She's still my special cat *Lucky!*

Shannon Lynn (11)
Magherafelt High School, Magherafelt

A Hallowe'en Poem

Hallowe'en is full of witches, scary faces,
Costumes and cauldrons.
Dressing up and trick or treating, these
We do on Hallowe'en night.

Nuts and oranges, apples too, dunking,
For these are great fun too.
Fireworks, rockets, sparklers, they're great,
Letting them off from eight till late.

Hallowe'en parties, oh what fun,
Meeting friends and their mums,
Just be careful when you are out,
There might be something scary about.

Matthew Hepburn (12)
Magherafelt High School, Magherafelt

Clock Face

Time keeps passing away
Right on through the day
'What time is it?' I say,
'It's time for school.
Don't be late or you will look a fool.'
I run for the bus cause I don't want to cause a fuss.

The clock strikes one and it's dinner time,
I'm so hungry and I don't feel fine,
Tick-tock the clock is ticking,
I don't have time for that chicken,
It's back to class,
I start to rush and move really fast.

The bell rings and it's the end of the school day,
I head for the bus and am on my way,
I walk through the door,
And I stare at the clock face,
Knowing in twelve hours time it starts all over again.

Scott Coles (11)
Magherafelt High School, Magherafelt

My Trip To Spain

I would like to go back to Spain,
Where the sun shines and it never rains.
It was fun to go to explore,
The rock pools at the shore.
Wearing a hat and shades made me cool,
I loved to swim and dive into the pool.
We had fun on the run with water guns,
Dinner, my favourite was chicken and chips.
A can of Coke made me lick my lips,
To end the day, a treat of ice cream,
Then time for bed and dream, dream, dream.

Andrew Lennox (12)
Magherafelt High School, Magherafelt

Summer

Summertime is here,
I give a big cheer,
Children are screaming,
And everyone is beaming.

No more school,
Everyone's in the pool
Splashing about
Nowhere is out of bounds.

The sun is out,
And everyone is about,
We are all at the beach,
And I hear the big screech.

Cooling down in the sun,
And there's no need to dream,
This is the last night,
And school is in sight.

Lynsey Yorke (13)
Magherafelt High School, Magherafelt

Hallowe'en

Hallowe'en is back again,
In another couple of weeks,
Everyone is getting ready,
To play trick or treat.

Everyone in funny costumes,
Scary ones too,
People going around knocking on doors,
Collecting money and food.

After that,
The fireworks begin,
Watching them go up so high,
That brightens up the sky.

Stacey Young (12)
Magherafelt High School, Magherafelt

The Dam

A cold and frosty morning
With just a hint of snow,
Ghostly shapes in the hedges
Everywhere we go.
The grass makes crackly noises
With each step as I walk,
My breath cold, comes out like smoke
With each word as I talk.
Along the path and through the trees,
Oh boy it's cold, excuse me, I sneeze,
A rabbit scurries off through the snow,
We must have really scared it,
For it can really go.
Nobody has been around this path,
For quite a while I think,
As we make our way through,
And here it is, the dam,
It's frozen like an ice rink.

Stephen Cochrane (11)
Magherafelt High School, Magherafelt

Christmas

Wake up, it's Christmas time,
Run downstairs screaming, shouting,
What's mine?
Tear open the wrapping,
Yes!
I got what I wanted,
Look, oh look Mum!
Congratulations, you got what you wanted,
Now come on breakfast time,
Mmm, bacon, sausages, pancakes, my favourite,
Gobble, gobble, I'm done, bye!
Vroom, vroom, bang, bang, clank, clank.

Alex Holgate (12)
Magherafelt High School, Magherafelt

The Night Of Hallowe'en

It was the night of Hallowe'en,
When all the children were in their beds,
The ghosts and ghouls came out to play,
Staggering out of their domains,
Awakening from their deadly slumber sleep.

It was the night of Hallowe'en,
When the fireworks went bang and crackle,
When the lights and sounds glittered in the sky,
The witch who cackles and pops,
Stirring her dreadful brew.

It was the night of Hallowe'en,
When the dogs barked in fright,
When the cats hid in fear,
The horseman galloped across the countryside,
Searching for his forgotten mangled head.

It was the night of Hallowe'en,
The trick or treaters were being egged
And the sparklers flickered and gleamed,
The werewolf provided through the city streets,
Stalking his prey for fresh blood.

It was the night of Hallowe'en,
When everybody was singing and dancing,
Not knowing the dangers lurking in the shadows,
Count Dracula is clambering out of the crypt which held him prisoner,
Scanning the area for his next victim, to be his wife.

It was the night of Hallowe'en.

Rebecca Austin (11)
Magherafelt High School, Magherafelt

Christmas Time

Christmas time is coming soon,
It's my favourite time of year,
People singing,
Church bells ringing,
Joy fills the air.

Log fires burning,
Young children wondering,
What Santa has for them,
Lights shining bright,
Late into the night,
Families snuggled up tight.

Thoughts of turkey, stuffing
And pies,
Smells from the kitchen,
Slowly arise,
Mum's busy cooking.

Presents from Granny,
Aunt and cousins,
Sit under the tree,
Waiting to be opened,
Could it be socks
Or maybe a toy?
Gifts for every girl and boy.

So let us celebrate this season,
With love, joy and peace,
And may we all find happiness
As we share this blessed time.

William McClenaghan (12)
Magherafelt High School, Magherafelt

How I Miss The Summer

How I miss the long nights,
How I miss flying kites,
All summer long we had great fun,
Playing happily in the sun.

Fishing in the sea,
Heaven to me,
Playing in the park,
Long into the dark.

Warm summer days,
I just drift away,
Walking on the beach,
An ice cream each.

But now that's gone,
But it will be back,
Summer will be coming again.

Gemma Young (12)
Magherafelt High School, Magherafelt

School Life

In the early days
I was quite amazed
At my new High School
With corridors like a maze.

Time has moved on
And I've settled in
I've made new friends
Who've shown me the trends.

I've got used to the teachers,
Learnt all the rules
Got used to all the bus rides
Which takes me to school.

Nicky Leslie (12)
Magherafelt High School, Magherafelt

Hallowe'en

When I think of Hallowe'en,
I think of
Dark, dark nights,
Witches and ghosts.
When I think of Hallowe'en,
I think of
The people who got burnt at the stake,
Witches being hung and tried.
When I think of Hallowe'en,
I think of
People dressed in spooky costumes.

Running, shouting, trick or treat,
Getting sweets, watching fireworks,
Filling the sky with light.

Frazer Lamont (12)
Magherafelt High School, Magherafelt

The Little Black Cat!

I walked up my garden path one night,
And something moved and gave me a fright,
I saw a shadow on the garden wall,
And saw two eyes which were very small.

I looked around,
And there I found,
A little black cat,
Which on the ground sat.

I picked it up and took it home,
To where it was safe and could roam,
It lay on my lap and there did sleep,
It didn't make one little noise not even one
Little peep.

Catherine Young (12)
Magherafelt High School, Magherafelt

Haunted House

Creak goes the door,
Crack goes the floor.

Groans and moans,
Sound like telephones.

Spiders on the wall,
Start to crawl.

I go up a hallway,
To a doorway.

Something gets out of bed,
It looks half-dead.

It has a green mean face
And a purple body.

Oh no! It's worst than a monster,
It's Granny in her green face cream,
And purple robe.

And this is her house!

Glenn Henry (12)
Magherafelt High School, Magherafelt

Hallowe'en

H aunted houses are haunted by ghosts,
A pples are ripe and people play dunking for apples,
L ots of children are off school,
L aughter is all around because everybody is having fun,
O ff everyone goes, trick or treating,
W itche's cats are miaowing in the light of the moon,
E veryone starts to tell ghost stories to scare their friends,
E xcitement is building up because children are
                              carving their pumpkins,
N ight owls and bats are hooting and screeching at
                       midnight and all the children are in their beds.

Natalie Johnston (12)
Magherafelt High School, Magherafelt

My Dog

When I get home from school,
My dog is there to play,
When I get home from school,
He wants to play all day.

When I get my homework done,
My dog wants his tea,
So I give him his tea,
And 10 minutes later, my mum shouts
'Tea!' to me.

My dog is getting tired,
So I take him up to bed,
And by half-past nine,
He has nodded his little head.

Now the dog is sleeping,
My homework is done,
We have had our fun,
It's time for me to go to bed.

Kirsty Lynn (11)
Magherafelt High School, Magherafelt

Autumn Days

A nother summer has gone by,
U nder trees the chestnuts lie,
T ime to hear the rustling of the leaves,
U nderneath my feet as I walk by,
M ore time indoors, less fun and play,
N ow autumn time is here.

D ark evenings are now near,
A nd the cold frosty mornings appear,
Y ellow leaves, they turn to brown,
S oon it will be Christmas time.

Gillian Brooks (12)
Magherafelt High School, Magherafelt

Hallowe'en

Hallowe'en is a time of year,
When all the children cry with fear,
Witches flying high in the sky,
Wizards casting spells,
Pumpkins all lit up,
With all their different faces.

Children dressing up,
Devils, witches and wizards,
Every type of creature,
At every single door,
Knock, knock, knock goes my door,
Then the Grim Reaper gives a roar,
Give them sweets,
They're sure to calm down,
Then off they'll go to another town.

'Trick or treat? Smell my feet.'
Is all that you can hear,
From dawn till dusk, doors are knocked,
'Trick or treat? Smell my feet.
Have you something nice to eat?
Knick-knock, knick-knock,
Argh! Argh! Argh! Argh! Argh!

Lauren Scott (12)
Magherafelt High School, Magherafelt

Arsenal

A rsenal is the best,
R ejoicing when they win the cup,
S hooting and they are great at it,
E ager to win the game,
N oisy as they come onto the field,
A nxious to get it finished,
L oving the fans when they come out.

Andrew Mitchell (12)
Magherafelt High School, Magherafelt

Hallowe'en

Hallowe'en night is spooky and scary
When darkness comes
Fireworks are bangin'.
Children are knocking on neighbour's doors
Trick or treat?
Getting sweets, fruit and nuts,
Witches are flying through the air,
With broomsticks and little black cats,
Ducking for apples,
As the bonfire burns,
Going to parties,
Dressing up,
As witches, devils and vampires too,
Telling stories of spooky houses and ghosts.
At the end of the night,
We all go to bed.

Aaron McLean (12)
Magherafelt High School, Magherafelt

Hallowe'en

Hallowe'en is a time of year,
That brings a lot of spooks and fear,
Fireworks go off in the sky,
Have you tried some pumpkin pie?
Look at all the lovely treats,
Some kids are dressed as ghosts in white sheets.
Ducking for apples, can you succeed?
It's not that hard when you take the lead,
Sparklers are pretty, all the different colours,
But watch out,
They can cause a lot of bother!
Pumpkins are alight at night,
And can give the children a fright.

Catherine Dempsey (12)
Magherafelt High School, Magherafelt

My School Poem

The ringing bell at 9.15am,
Run quickly as you can.
You're late for class again, oh no!
Wait, who cares, it's not the end of the world,
Pick up the pencil and start to write.

The bell rings again after three periods, it's break time,
Go outside and play with your friends.
The ringing bell rings again,
Better get to class.

After six periods of fun, fun, fun,
It's time to go home.
At least we have no homework to do,
So let's have more fun.

Jessica McKeown (11)
Magherafelt High School, Magherafelt

Autumn

Leaves are falling to the ground,
Floating down without a sound
Walking through the leafy paths
They make a lovely scrunching mass.
Chilling winds come blowing fast
And make a terrible whistling blast.
Little creatures hiding go,
Before the fall of winter snow.
Hallowe'en is drawing near,
It fills our minds with dread and fear.
Apple tart is quite a treat,
If you make it nice and sweet.
Witches, goblins and ghosts stare,
With their awful heartless glare.

Esther Redfern (11)
Magherafelt High School, Magherafelt

Jumpy, Jolly Friends

I have a lot of really good friends,
We're all in 8A1,
We met each other on that first day,
And now we've loads of fun.

The seven of us are jumpy and jolly,
And we play lots of games,
Like stick the sticker on someone's back,
Now would you like to hear their names?

We have Nadine, Rebecca and Becky too,
We are all such good mates,
But then there's Stephanie, Tasha and Julie,
Now Julie will crack the plates.

Stephanie's the mad one in the group,
With Becky there to follow,
And don't ask Julie a question,
'Cause she's too many Aero bars to swallow.

Now Nadine and Rebecca are the quiet ones,
They'll never scream and shout,
But you would hardly ever hear them,
With me and Stephanie about.

Judith Johnston (11)
Magherafelt High School, Magherafelt

My Day

I help my daddy every day,
To feed the cows and give them hay.
To cut the crops and bring them in,
Before the winter storms begin.

I help my mummy every night,
To watch my sisters and not let them fight.
My brother too wants me to play,
Before we end a happy day.

David Forsythe (11)
Magherafelt High School, Magherafelt

My Dad's Two Dogs

My dad's two dogs are completely mad,
He does nothing but shout and shout that they're bad.
When he lets them out in the morning they jump,
And he shouts in the evening, sit down or you'll get a thump.

My dad's two dogs play in the yard,
I try to catch them but it's very hard.
They play with two balls and a piece of stick,
When you try to take them from them
                            they give you are lick.

My dad's two dogs love to go for a walk,
Their favourite place to go is the lough.
Once they get there, they jump in and splash,
And when they get home they both get a wash.

Jill Hassan (11)
Magherafelt High School, Magherafelt

Winter

Winter is a time of year,
When some bad weather comes,
Snow, rain and hailstones too,
Which sometimes cause bad accidents.

When winter comes,
We wrap up well,
In boots, coats, scarves and gloves,
And then we have some fun as well,
On sleighs and maybe skis.

In the winter Christmas comes,
And we have lots of fun,
Opening presents and eating dinners,
And also gathering with family.

Leanne Carleton (11)
Magherafelt High School, Magherafelt

Oh What A Beautiful Saturday

Oh what a beautiful Saturday,
Oh what a lovely weekend,
Oh what a brilliant performance,
United are making amends.

Time for a change of our tactics,
Time for a change to our play,
Time for Giggs' new contract
As that lad was superb today.

So now we are playing on Saturday,
So now we are off to Liverpool,
So now all supporters are asking,
'What if United should fail?

Continue to keep up the spirits,
Continue to keep up the fun,
Continue to keep on supporting
United are now on a run.

Daniel Boone (11)
Magherafelt High School, Magherafelt

Hallowe'en

On Hallowe'en night,
Monsters give us a terrible fright,
There's a robot with a baseball bat,
And a witch on a broom with her shrieking cat.

The werewolf is howling,
Inside my dog is growling,
There's also an ugly fly,
I'm not telling you a lie.

There's ghosts flying about,
They're making a loud shout,
The fireworks are making very loud bangs,
And the vampires are showing their fangs.

Helen Donaldson (13)
Magherafelt High School, Magherafelt

The Haunted House

It stands all alone,
Moon reflecting bright light,
Shining off its tall roof,
In the pitch-dark of the night.

It is three stories high,
Built way back in 1804,
My hands are shaking drastically,
As I open the old stiff door.

I slowly go inside and
Look cautiously around,
It's so eerily quiet,
My breathing the only sound.

Proceeding up the staircase,
I remember all the tales,
And suddenly I wonder,
Who could hear my wails?

What has made me come?
Whatever brought me here?
To prove the folks wrong
There is nothing to fear.

I reach the third floor,
I stare in awe at the view,
This was once a home,
The stories are not true.

I leave three hours later,
And take down the sign,
It's been for sale too long,
This historic house is now mine.

Claire Riddell (12)
Magherafelt High School, Magherafelt

The Famine That Hit Ireland In 1845

This word famine - what does it mean?
It means hardship and poverty,
for many a one.

Families left homeless, nothing to wear.
Poor clothing and sometimes,
their feet were bare.

Scarcely food on the table,
was little to eat.
Many were dying
in every street.

The potato came from
a land far away.
In Ireland it was eaten
practically every day.

They could be big or small,
blue or white
and could be eaten by day or night!

A field of potatoes,
is a wonderful sight,
until along came a disease that we now call Blight.

It was and still is a horrible disease,
carried along on the slightest breeze.
Very quickly it can travel far and wide,
covering the entire countryside.

This really hit home in 1845,
leaving many people barely alive!

Dawn McMullan (13)
Magherafelt High School, Magherafelt

Hatred

Some people hate me
Some people love me
But now the people that loved me, hate me
And so do I.

One thing that's all it takes,
To make their hearts, shut on the brakes,
I know deep down there's love there somewhere,
But when they look at me, my heart they see
I feel disappointment of what I've turned out to be.

Happy times are all I think,
I do think of these,
When the people I love turn to drink,
We hate to see this, everyone does,
Then we think, *is it because?*

I hate something in turn,
One punch that's all I yearn,
He drives me insane,
I'd love to show him real pain.

The one thing they remember,
Is something I try to forget.

The names aren't real,
But based on the truth,
But when you yourself find this hatred for one person
Hang onto it,
'Cause it makes the good times meaningful,
So hold onto the hatred,
It will serve you well.

Adam Kells (12)
Magherafelt High School, Magherafelt

A Midnight Walk

Sitting by the fire all cosy and warm,
I knew it was bedtime and I would sleep till dawn.
My dad shouted, *'Bedtime!'* and without a peep
I put on my pyjamas and fell sound asleep.

Suddenly I was walking under a starry sky,
And in the middle of the forest I heard a cry!
I looked all around me but no one was there,
Then all of a sudden I began to stare.

There in the clearing was a big brown bear,
He was eating biscuits and asked *me* to share,
I walked over slowly and timidly sat on a rock,
And to my amazement he started to talk.

He told me his story of why he was there,
To find someone who he knew would really care.
In the forest where he had lived so long,
His only friend had been an ugly green frog.

He needed a girlfriend, a bear to care,
All of his friends thought he was a *square,*
He needed someone to dance with even for a dare,
He asked me to help him find a cute bear,
One with a pink ribbon in her curly brown hair.

We searched the forest high and low,
And then we saw her with her pink bow,
She looked at Bob and she gave him a nod,
And I said to myself, *'Clever old Bob.'*

I don't know what happened to Bob and his bear,
Because the next thing I knew my alarm clock blew.
Was my walk a dream? And had I really shared,
Biscuits and cookies with that silly old bear?

Leah Mulholland (11)
Magherafelt High School, Magherafelt

Hallowe'en Night

It's Hallowe'en night,
And everything just seems to be a
Fright!
Fireworks going off here and there,
Everybody's running around
Looking full of fear,
All you can see is little children eating,
Then you know that they'd just been
Tricker or treating,
Everybody's talking about witches,
Some even say they hide in ditches,
Well! That's Hallowe'en for you,
It's just full of people screaming
Boo!

Alanna Johnston (13)
Magherafelt High School, Magherafelt

All About Maize

Maize is a crop,
That feeds the stock.
In October the farmer,
Gives it the chop.

The big machine,
With its mighty roar,
Through the fields it does soar.
Cutting, chopping as it goes,
Into the trailers it does blow.

To the pit it does go,
Tipping up very slow,
Then when covered it will be,
Fed to the animals in February.

Richard Patterson (12)
Magherafelt High School, Magherafelt

Hallowe'en Night

Hallowe'en night,
Was a marvellous sight,
Trick or treating,
Sneaky creepy,
Witches flying,
Children crying,
People all dressed up,
People blown up,
Fireworks banging,
Ghosts are hanging,
Bonfires sparkling,
Nuts are cracking,
And that is the
End of
Hallowe'en night!

Kyle Irwin (12)
Magherafelt High School, Magherafelt

Hallowe'en

Hallowe'en the night of fun,
Bats above our heads and ghosts.
In the shadows goblins walking the streets,
And black cats flying on broomsticks,
The werewolves at night,
Scary spirits back from the dead.
People with sweets ready for the trick or treaters,
Vampires and Dracula ready for blood,
Mummies and zombies walking around the graveyards,
Witches and spells.
Haunted houses with spooky monsters,
Pumpkins on the doorsteps,
This is *Hallowe'en!*

Samuel Watterson (11)
Magherafelt High School, Magherafelt

My Dad Says . . .

My dad says,
'Get up for school,
Get dressed,
Get your breakfast,
Get in the car.'

My dad says,
'Do your homework,
Tidy your room,
See to your ponies,
Brush the yard.'

My dad says,
'Get your dinner,
Get your PJs on,
Get ready for school tomorrow,
Brush your teeth,
Get to bed,
Turn out the light.'

My dad says,
'Good night,
Sleep tight,
Don't let the bedbugs bite!'

Stephen Brown (11)
Magherafelt High School, Magherafelt

Hallowe'en

Witches, brooms and bubbling cauldrons,
Spiders, ghosts and skeletons,
Goblins, mummies and Frankenstein,
Don't be surprised if you see them around.

Hallowe'en is spooky and haunted,
What fun we have when we fancy dress,
Parties and fireworks and spooky spirits
What fun it is to celebrate.

Rachel Hassan (11)
Magherafelt High School, Magherafelt

The Famine!

It all began in 1845,
When a lot of Irish people were alive,
The English people took the food,
'Cause of the famine the crops were no good,
The Irish got hungry and started dying,
And in the ditches people were lying.

It all got worse in 1847,
When most people ended up in Heaven.
People prayed for God to help them,
But instead God sent the evicting men,
The famine was also called The Blight,
When it first came it gave people a fright.

In 1849,
I said my goodbyes for the last time,
I was setting sail to the United States,
I brought everything even my plates,
The sailing was very rough,
I had said goodbye to my life which was tough!

Katrina Steele (13)
Magherafelt High School, Magherafelt

Hallowe'en

Every year at Hallowe'en,
I would give a big, loud scream.
I would trick or treat,
And eat lots of sweets,
Every year at Hallowe'en.

We would hang up decorations,
And have lots of celebrations.
Fire fireworks into the air,
Dunk for apples here and there,
Every year at Hallowe'en.

April Shiels (11)
Magherafelt High School, Magherafelt

I've Got A . . .

I've got a dog called Spot,
Who thinks he's very hot.

I've got a horse called Lee,
Who has a wobbly knee.

I've got a hamster called Rod,
Who always acts like a cod.

I've got a bird called Norm,
Who thinks he's an alarm.

I've got a fish called Bob,
Who looks a bit like my doorknob.

I've got a cat called Cheeky,
Who of course is very sneaky.

I've got a rabbit called Nash,
Who you would think was part of the trash.

Leanne Sloss (11)
Magherafelt High School, Magherafelt

The Dogs Behind The Dustbin

Down behind the dustbin,
I met a dog called Tom,
'Do you live here?' I said,
'No, I live on a farm.'

Down behind a dustbin,
I met a dog called Sue,
'What are you doing here?' I said,
'I can't find my friends, can you?'

Down behind a dustbin,
I met a dog called Miller,
'What are you doing?' I said,
'I'm just looking for my dinner.'

Trevor Jordan (11)
Magherafelt High School, Magherafelt

Hallowe'en

The shops are full of things for Hallowe'en,
Costumes, fireworks, streamers, spiders or brooms.
Huge pumpkins ready to be carved out,
Bags of sweets for trick or treating.

On Hallowe'en night the sky will light up,
With all the bright colours from the fireworks.
Screeching rockets bursting into all the colours of the rainbow.
Fireworks with names like Spiral Fountain, Cascading River, or
Shower of Light.

Large bonfires burning bright,
Children with sparklers and lanterns,
Warm clothes for the cold night.
After the fun then into the house,
For spooky Hallowe'en food.

Mark Purvis (11)
Magherafelt High School, Magherafelt

The Country Comes Alive

Little flowers wake up and dress the garden,
Green grass sits up and looks at the sun,
Chestnut trees throw off their clothes,
Houses crying, 'We need painting!'
Windows covered with wood, 'It's dark, they cry.'
Hungry black bins gobbling all the litter,
Cracking paths screaming, 'Don't walk on us it hurts,'
Fence boards all lined up like soldiers, 'Left, right, *march!*'
Thorn roses all cut down below,
Swings, swinging back and forward yelling, 'Stop us!'
Garage doors slamming, 'Ouch, ouch.'
The sun has gone to bed, 'Goodnight,' she sighs.

Rebekah Clements (11)
Magherafelt High School, Magherafelt

Autumn

As we look out
And get ready for school
The rain it lies
In the yard in a pool.

The tall trees swaying
Back and forth
By the cold wind that blows
From the north.

It's starting to rain
The sunflowers are dying
Except for one
And it's just lying.

The horse looks cold
As she peers over the wire
She'd be warmer inside
If she could stand by the fire.

The time it changes
The nights get longer
As autumn sets in
The wind gets stronger.

Jillian Jones (11)
Magherafelt High School, Magherafelt

Shopping

Looking at all the rails,
Wondering if this will go with my new nails,
Having wondered what to wear.
I am scared I'll look like a bear.

As I walk to the next shop,
I spot this really cool top.
Should I buy it or leave well alone?
Maybe I'll keep my money and buy a large cone!

Deborah Wilkinson (12)
Magherafelt High School, Magherafelt

Stop!

Just have a little think,
Before you drop that paper,
We'll be living in a world of mess,
Sooner or later,

My parents always told me,
To put litter in a bin,
Because to leave it lying on the ground,
Is quite a big sin!

When you go into the shop,
And you buy yourself a treat,
Always put the wrappers in the bin,
Don't leave them on the street!

So heed this little message,
Don't leave rubbish on the ground,
You'll see the world a better place,
Where no rubbish can be found!

Ruth Scott (14)
Magherafelt High School, Magherafelt

Does No One Care

Dead and dying,
People wailing, children crying,
And all the time the hunger gnaws,
It's got our stomachs in its claws.
Even the sun has lost its warmth.

The potatoes rot darkly in the earth,
The pots lie empty on the hearth,
Heavy hopelessness . . .
Is it true? Does no one care?

Jill Henderson (13)
Magherafelt High School, Magherafelt

The Famine In Ireland!

In Ireland the potato crop failed in 1845
It was hard for the people to survive
In fact, a lot of people died
And I'm sure many, many cried.

Some took sick and died from TB
Others fled to countries across the sea
On 'coffin ships' they sailed away
Some as far as the USA.

Food kitchens were opened by the society of friends
But no help at all did the government lend
The poor and the sick to the workhouses were sent
That's where their last days on Earth were spent.

Do we ever thank God for the food that we eat?
Remember there are many with an empty plate
Don't ever take your food for granted
or say to your parents, 'That's not what I wanted!'

Stephanie Sloss (13)
Magherafelt High School, Magherafelt

Friends

Friends, friends we need them all,
If we didn't we wouldn't go to the mall.
We go outside have a laugh,
I come back in and have a bath.
We go to the park, we see a dog,
I go back home there's lots of fog.
Cars fly past, the lights are on,
Another day has almost gone.
Friends, friends we need them all,
Unless I have no one at all.

Nicola Bamford (12)
Magherafelt High School, Magherafelt

My Name is Misty

My name is Misty, I am but three
My eyes are swollen, I cannot see
I must be stupid, I must be bad
What else could have made them so mad?

I wish I was good, I wish I weren't ugly
Then maybe my mammy would still want to hug me.
I can't speak at all, I can't have a flaw
Or else I'm locked up all day long.

When I wake up I'm all alone
The house is in darkness, my folks aren't home.
When my mammy comes I'll try to be nice
So maybe I'll just get one hiding tonight.

I am 'an accident', that's the words
For time and time again that phrase I've heard
I'm quiet now, I hear a car
My dad is home from the local bar.

I hear him curse . . . my name he calls
I throw myself against the walls
Oh please Lord, it's much too late
His face is twisted into utter hate.

Oh God just let it end . . .

He finally stops and heads for the door
While I lie there motionless and lifeless on the floor.
My name is Misty, I am but three
Tonight my daddy murdered me.

Stacey Henry (12)
Magherafelt High School, Magherafelt

Truck Show

The dates have been set,
The hard work begins,
The name of the game,
Is to see who wins.

Drivers do their day's work,
And at night they do more,
Inside and out, their lorries they clean,
Right from the roof and down to the floor.

Polishing and dusting their pride and joy,
This is when the man behaves like a boy,
Just for the weekend the work's left behind,
The lorries are on show, that's all that's on their mind.

On Saturday morning, the King's Hall is the place,
Each driver will drive in at a very slow pace,
The lorries are shining - a sight to behold,
For truckers and followers, both young and old.

So many categories for the judges to see,
Old trucks, new trucks, interiors and livery,
The weekend is nearly over, the decisions are made,
Whose lorry has won prizes, whose reached the grade?

The truckers and families gather in the great hall,
All eagerly waiting for their name to be called,
For Ashlea Haulage - that's my dad's firm you see,
We got three prizes, and I smiled with glee!

Matthew Stewart (13)
Magherafelt High School, Magherafelt

Who Am I?

Who am I?
Now let me see . . .
There are many sides to me.

In the morning when I wake,
Fixing my hair often makes me late.

After breakfast of eggs and tea,
You will see a different side of me!

When I arrive at my school,
I'm looking fresh and really cool.

Lessons start I concentrate,
As I work hard to seal my fate.

Lunch and break help me unwind,
Which takes the hard work off my mind.

Sports and play practise there's lots to do,
To make a better player out of you.

Home for dinner, cannot wait,
Homework to do before it's late.

Feed my dog and feline friends,
And that's the way my day ends.

Up the stairs I haste to bed,
With many new thoughts in my head.

Before too long I'm fast asleep,
Until I hear the alarm clock beep.

Chloe Anderson (13)
Magherafelt High School, Magherafelt

Friends

We all have lots of friends
We need them all the time
They're there for us to talk to
To listen when we're down.

Our friends are very special
Sometimes we giggle, sometimes we fight
We always trust each other
And we'll stay friends alright.

We like to dress in the latest gear
We dance and sing without a fear
Sometimes off to the Odyssey we go
To enjoy the latest show.

I'm glad to have good friends
At least I'm not alone
I know we'll all be happy
Whether together or alone.

Carolyn Moore (11)
Magherafelt High School, Magherafelt

Hallowe'en

Hallowe'en is in autumn time,
When the weather is not so hot.
The leaves are falling off the trees,
And it is getting dark a lot.
Hallowe'en is a spooky time
When your heart could nearly stop.
'Trick or treat?' is what we hear.
The children shouting in the street,
I'm glad you are all here
For this spooky time of year.
Spirits in the air, so please beware,
Watch yourself and take good care.

Timothy Paul (11)
Magherafelt High School, Magherafelt

Hallowe'en

Bonfires blazing bright,
People in the night,
Children having fun,
Hallowe'en has just begun.

Fireworks going off everywhere,
They're all lighting up the sky.
Rockets shooting across the sky,
Little stars falling through the air,
Disappearing before your eyes.

Angeline Evans (12)
Magherafelt High School, Magherafelt

Colours

Red means anger,
Hot fiery-tempered anger.
It means embarrassment,
Red-cheeked embarrassment.

Yellow means happiness,
Friendly, joyful happiness.
It means light,
Light from the sun's long warming rays.

Blue means calm,
Peaceful, sincere and calm.
It means water,
Water from the huge body we call 'The Sea'.

Green means jealousy,
Ungrateful, greedy jealousy.
It means wildlife,
Green grass, part of the beautiful wildlife.

White means peace,
No wars, no conflict, pure peace.
It means soap,
Cleansing away our impurity.

Lisa Gannon (14)
St Fanchea's College, Enniskillen

Autumn Glow

Yellow, red, green, brown
Leaves a-floating to the ground.
Funny shapes and sizes too,
The wind blows them from their home.

Autumn is a special time
When fruit and berries grow.
Red, fat strawberries and blackberries
So juicy and sweet to taste.

Autumn makes me glow inside,
The rain makes musical sounds.
The beautiful colours of the fireworks
Scare away the sun as it tries to say, 'Hello.'

Autumn fills me with a glow.

Shauna Fee (14)
St Fanchea's College, Enniskillen

A Place To Call My Own

I'm told that I can be someone; it's hard to think I can,
Because I'm not even sure of the person that I am.
Laid down in the darkness, lying all alone,
I close my eyes and dream of a place to call my own.

Sometimes I feel so empty like I'm breaking up inside,
No explanation for this feeling something in me must have died.
I can't make any sense of all the passing days,
I don't understand why I feel this way; maybe it's just a phase.

But then there are days I feel so great nothing could put me down,
A smile is stuck upon my face you'll never see a frown.
They're the days I love and I will never let slip away.
I'll find a place to call my own I'll find that place some day.

Stephanie O'Neill (14)
St Fanchea's College, Enniskillen

The Blue Moon

The blue moon
Sits upon the hill.
It kindles fiercely
Yet is so still.

Wide eyes set upon it
With such delight,
Oh how it brightens up
The sparkling night.

It kisses the stars,
It softens the rain.
It looks so delicate
In its heavenly frame.

You can hear the wind whisper
As it passes by,
See the moon as it twinkles
In your loved one's eyes.

Bronagh McCahery (13)
St Fanchea's College, Enniskillen

War

War is such a terrible thing
It causes wave after wave of sadness.
Every day brings something else,
But very rarely gladness.

War is something I can't control
It's something I don't like.
I can never get my head around it,
Yet it's always present in our lives.

When war is all over
Only then can mad men see
That God was watching over us
Over him, over you, over me.

Hannah McKiernan (14)
St Fanchea's College, Enniskillen

Alone In My Thoughts

Alone I sit and ponder my thoughts.
Away and hidden in the lonely dark.
The cool, aloof breeze whispers at my face
As I sit and dwell in my special place.

The water trickles peacefully down,
The fish make hardly a ripple.
I notice my reflection as it starts to rain;
And my image is thrown into distortion
As I sit in my special place.

Nothing for comfort just the dark clouds
That now hang over my head.
The birds fly for shelter,
And as the rain gets heavier and heavier
I flee my special place.

Maeve McKenna (14)
St Fanchea's College, Enniskillen

Absent Love

Forever in my heart you will be,
A vague memory I long to keep.
The little bit of time we had together
Is gone, but not forever.

Why did you go? Why did you leave?
Mourning for you my family and I grieved
As you were lowered down underground
I realise that your time has come, you're no longer around.

I sit in silence and say a little prayer
Just to let you know
My love is always there.

Forever in my heart you shall be
The one I love, but just can't see.

Sheila Woods (13)
St Fanchea's College, Enniskillen

No More War

Our world is destroyed
With war and with crime.
Lay down your weapons,
Now is the time.

It's gone too far,
You'll regret it some day
When all of your family
Have passed away.

As the coffin is lowered
Then tears you will cry,
As you know how it feels
For someone so close to die.

God made us all
To care and to love.
So, stop the war and
Release the caged dove.

Una Burns (13)
St Fanchea's College, Enniskillen

Can Anyone Hear Me?

I'm calling out for help
No one can hear me
Screaming to be heard
No one can hear me.

I don't want this feeling anymore
No one can hear me
I want to tell someone
No one can hear me.

I get up the courage
To talk my problem through
My burden is shared
My voice is heard.

Aimee Johnston (12)
St Mary's Grammar School, Magherafelt

The Scary Ride

Collecting money for the rides and food,
I am definitely in a good mood.

Waiting in the big, long queue,
My stomach has butterflies, but just a few.

Getting on the ride now I'm not that keen,
Scared looks from the adults and also some teens.

Here it goes, oh no!
I shouldn't have eaten before my go.

My belly's gone jelly, my hair's a disaster,
But this horrid ride keeps going faster and faster.

Finally it stops into a halt
And I get off fast as a lightning bolt.

I definitely am not going on that ride again,
But maybe this ride, *The Temple of Pain.*

Caroline McKenna (11)
St Mary's Grammar School, Magherafelt

A Forest Walk

Evergreens reaching towards the sky
A little squirrel scampers by
An autumn carpet on the ground
Leaves of yellow, red and brown
The call of pheasants far and near
And what is that, a pair of deer
Old wood lies like rotten bones
Surrounded by berries, acorns and cones
Waves gushing on the shore
Ducks, swans and birds galore
Peace and quiet fills the air
Crowds and traffic go elsewhere.

Zoë Robb (11)
St Mary's Grammar School, Magherafelt

Gently Falling

I looked out in the morning
And to my great surprise
Everything that I could see was white before my eyes.

Lovely little flakes of snow hovered round and round
They floated gently in the breeze and settled on the ground.

I dressed as quickly as I could, slipped quietly down the stairs,
Disappeared out the door into the frosty air.

I played all day, I made a slide it was very cold
Then Roisin hit me with a snowball, yes, I know she's very bold.

I made a great big snowman with a carrot for a nose,
He looked so good with coal for eyes, dressed up in Daddy's clothes.

When darkness fell that evening and all the prayers were said
Mummy gave me some hot chocolate and sent me up to bed.

I looked out the next morning and to my great dismay
All that lovely snow had somehow gone away.

Grainne Cassidy (12)
St Mary's Grammar School, Magherafelt

The Haunted Graveyard

One foggy Hallowe'en night,
It was five minutes to the witching hour,
Young children were out, trick or treating,
Suddenly one tiptoed up and knocked on the church door,
Then the ghosts rose out of their graves
And circled round the young child,
They started to chant a song,
The young child started to scream,
He started to run and dodge round the gravestones.
While the ghosts followed him,
He ran round the graveyard till one o'clock,
That marked the end of the witching hour
And the ghosts returned to their graves.

Andrew Keenan (13)
St Mary's Grammar School, Magherafelt

Edendork

Edendork
A village two miles from Coalisland,
And three miles from Dungannon;
Peaceful and quiet throughout the land,
With a fresh country smell;
Up a small lane lay a cottage,
Lined with ivy and vines,
Surrounded by fields of corn, barley and hay,
Like an open prairie in a distant land;
Winter, cold and dull,
With snow, sleet and hail,
A white carpet lay across the fields
And the robin redbreast sings.
Holly covered in snow,
Distinct by red berries,
Looking at my surroundings I said,
'This is a memory to keep;'
In the cool breeze of a warm summer,
The birds chirp and sing,
Listening quietly for any rustling
And a squirrel peeps up from a tree.
Yellow fields untouched and unmoved
And on the horizon some small rabbits jerked;
Clip-clop, clip-clop, a magnificent beast,
The horse behind took me breathless,
Jolting back to view this splendid sight,
Touching the hair was like touching silk,
So smooth and fine along my hand.
After the moment's silence, the horse trotted away;
On the top of the lane,
A rickety gate of rusted iron,
The boundary of the lane and hillside,
Climbing over I landed on a squelching patch
And at the peak of the climb,
I sat to watch the superior sight.
Lough Neagh's coast and further on,
Sunset drew near and just above The Sperrins,
Was the golden orange sun.

Soon the day becomes night,
I leave this unprovoked village;
Two miles from Coalisland
And three miles from Dungannon.

Gary Leung (13)
St Mary's Grammar School, Magherafelt

The Disappearing Scene

The sunset rose like a beacon of hope
Around the doom and the gloom of the night
Illuminating the cold mountain tops blue
Though the cold prickled against my skin
It could not freeze the warmth of my heart

Surrounded by the encircling arms of the fir trees
Closing in around me waiting to pounce
The city lights twinkling below my feet
Like a swarm of fireflies
I was the queen bee watching my drones at work

Crunch was the sound that drove my soul from me
Up I rose from the ground and ran as if possessed by a demon
Over rotten logs, branches whipping at my face
My blood pumping, the adrenaline flowing through me
Closer, closer the noise still ringing in my ears

Whence to a clearing I came
Like a large bald patch in a thick head of hair
Monsters with teeth of steel *chomping, crushing* and
Crashing
Birds squawking and screeching, fleeing their homes
The peace, the scenery, the creatures and the tranquillity
All gone.

Charlene Tennyson (13)
St Mary's Grammar School, Magherafelt

Scramblers

The sound is deafening
It hurts your ears
It is so loud
You begin to fear
Will they crash?
Will they not?
It is so fast
You begin to get hot
Then suddenly a smash
Parts go everywhere
He is rushed to hospital
The opposition sneers
The race is yellow-flagged
The racers all slow down
They don't want to end up like him
Looking like a clown.

Emmet McGuigan (12)
St Mary's Grammar School, Magherafelt

The Coral Reef

Deep under the sea
The fish frightened and flustered
Fly about the coral reef finding a hiding place
The word is spreading fast
The big, bad, basking shark was on its way and fast!
The fish saw the devastating destruction
The shark had left behind
It was such a horrible thing to find
The poor fish swam in silence
Mourning in their grief
As they saw in front of them
A destroyed coral reef!

Catherine O'Neill (12)
St Mary's Grammar School, Magherafelt

Christmas Eve

Fairy lights twinkling
Wrapping paper crinkling
Christmas crackers crackling
While the children are cackling

Spiky holly on the wreath
Children so excited that they can hardly breathe
Stockings on the fireplaces
Hanging on by their laces.

Snow is falling on the ground
Whitewashed floorboards all around
School nativity plays have a large cast
Santa Claus is coming
The children go to bed
Sleeping with presents
Dancing in their heads.

Terrie Duffin (12)
St Mary's Grammar School, Magherafelt

The Rain

How it pitters rapidly,
How it patters happily!
Along my windowpane.

In my cosy house I sit,
And watch the hurling rain,
Against my windowpane!

In showers of sadness,
In winds of badness!
It hisses by my windowpane.

Trickles, splashes, sparkles, glitters!
As rough as the crashing sea,
How it drives me insane!

Sarah McKenna (12)
St Mary's Grammar School, Magherafelt

The Cheetah

He ran across the vast savannah,
A yellow and black blob speeding past.
His feet barely touched the ground,
You could tell he was very fast.

He pounded after his prey ahead,
An unsuspecting deer eating away.
Unaware of the danger behind,
The deer had been led astray.

He pounced upon the young beauty
And ripped its flesh to shreds.
He finished off his bloody meal
And then returned to bed.

By now you should know what I'm talking about,
His main feature is he's very fast.
Yes he is a cheetah,
A yellow and black blob speeding past.

Sara Newe (13)
St Mary's Grammar School, Magherafelt

My Dog

I have a dog,
His name is Roy,
His fur is white,
He is a boy.

He likes to eat,
He likes to play,
He's very lazy,
He sleeps all day.

He barks a lot,
He fights with cats,
He's very nice,
He's very fat.

Michaela Donaghy (13)
St Mary's Grammar School, Magherafelt

Lonely Autumn

As I sat on the crunching leaves,
The squirrels and dormice
Danced around my knees.

Mice and hedgehogs,
Badgers too,
All contributed to blocking out my lonely view.

It was like the animals
Had joined together,
In this stimulating, vivid weather.

I used to think I was all on my own,
And now I know I'm not alone.

'Cause out there somewhere,
In the autumnal trees,
Whistles the calm and gentle breeze.

Eiméar McCollum (11)
St Mary's Grammar School, Magherafelt

Hallowe'en

It's time again
To trick or treat, to have great fun
To shout and scream,
'All my fireworks are done!'

To dress up as witches
Go to fancy dress
Have a great time
Dracula is a pest.

Playing with apples is what we like to do
Cooking, eating and catching them
Is a fun thing to do
Dunking, making apple pie.
We enjoy Hallowe'en so much!

Helen Close (13)
St Mary's Grammar School, Magherafelt

Winter Showers

Pitter-patter, pitter-patter,
That's how it starts off,
It trickles down the window so easily,
If only it would stay like that.

Crash! Crash! Crash!
Now this is the beginning,
The wind hitting you, smack,
If only it would stay like that.

Bang! Bang! Bang!
Now I am scared,
The thunder growling,
The lightning screaming,
If only it would go away.

Slowly, slowly, slowly,
This is it, over,
The wind is whistling,
The rain is sprinkling,
If only, if only, if only.

Sarah O'Donnell (12)
St Mary's Grammar School, Magherafelt

One Of The Crowd

When you're the only one left
And the night has turned cold
Look to the sky to see
What the future holds.

Those twinkling stars
Glistening all around
Brings comfort to those
Lost, still not found.

Your head is a-buzz
With a message that stands clear
Stand up and shout
Look at me, over here!

Don't let yourself be
Just one of the crowd
Make a name for yourself
Do yourself proud.

Grace McKenna (13)
St Mary's Grammar School, Magherafelt

Hallowe'en

The sun is setting,
Darkness is falling near.
The masks and costumes are coming out,
Young children are in fear.
The moon is bright and full,
A spectacular background,
For the many fireworks in the sky.
The witches get their black cats
And fly their broomsticks way up high.
A time for trick or treating,
Doors just pass us by.
Hallowe'en is ending,
Children don't want to say goodbye.
They travel home into their beds,
Tucked up nice and warm,
Hoping that the monsters,
Don't do them any harm.

Maria Crozier (12)
St Mary's Grammar School, Magherafelt

Awesome October

I see lots of colourful trees,
Red, brown, amber and green,
Swaying in the autumn breeze,
What a beautiful scene.

Animals everywhere searching frantically for food,
Squirrels, badgers and the occasional hedgehog,
It puts us in a Hallowe'en mood,
Children playing as they should.

Hallowe'en is coming, get the carving kit out,
Scary pumpkins and ghostly ghouls,
Give us a fright,
At midnight.

As blind as a bat, as sly as a cat,
What will you dress up as?
Will you wear a cape or a hat?
Whatever you wear, take care
And have a happy Hallowe'en and an
Awesome October!

Megan Scullion (13)
St Mary's Grammar School, Magherafelt

Different

Everyone is different, you and me
When you read this poem you will see.

I have green eyes, you may have blue
I am quite tall, could be taller than you.

I play the piano and the violin
You might not play anything.

I live in a place called County Derry
You might live in County Kerry.

I like art and dislike maths
You might like science, drawing graphs.

I could read all day long!
But you might prefer to sing a song!

I hope now you can see how different we are,
But you can only be yourself to be a star!

We all have talents they show who we are,
So use them wisely and you will go far!

Aoife McVey (11)
St Mary's Grammar School, Magherafelt

The Seasons

The countryside is beautiful, in autumn and in spring,
When you wake up in the morning and hear the birds sing.
Autumn's howling wind with the rustling of the leaves,
The soft cold feel of nature's fresh breeze.
The summer mornings with the sun and haze,
School's out - happy days
Longer evenings, we play all night
School for now is out of sight.
Smiling faces, the craic is great,
The next kick of the ball could decide our fate.
The whistle's gone. The game's at an end,
Our tired bones are now on the mend.
The snow is falling, this can only mean one thing . . .
Christmas is here and the carol singers sing.
The shops are busy, everyone's going mad,
When Christmas Day comes, I'll be so glad.
Spring's here, training has already begun,
We check the paper to see who has lost or won.
We train real hard and play with pride,
To make our team the greatest side.

Gerard Kearney (12)
St Mary's Grammar School, Magherafelt

Nightmare

As snowflakes flutter through the sky,
I let out a quiet sigh.

When that white blanket covered the ground,
That is when I heard that unusual sound.

The sound of silence, I could hear,
It felt as though I had nothing to fear.

But as I lie here in my bed,
Approaches that creature that I dread.

When I close my eyes and go to sleep,
Through the darkness of my nightmares it will creep.

It haunts me each and every night,
It is the most petrifying sight.

With hair like fire and eyes like coal,
It chills me to my very soul.

I can only hope that some day,
This horrible creature will go away.

But until then all I can do,
Is pass this tale on to you.

Daniel Hart (13)
St Mary's Grammar School, Magherafelt

Ambitions

Ambitions, ambitions, what will I be?
A nurse, a vet or on the TV
A TV presenter, an actress, a star
With all of my talents I could really go far

A doctor, a dentist or a pharmacist
I am never going to see the end of this list
I like to count money - I could work in a bank
I could be a builder with my old grandad Frank.

A teacher, a teacher - I'll be forever at school
A professional hairdresser, now that's really cool
An accountant, oh no, that would be boring
I bet you by lunchtime, I'd probably be snoring.

A designer for Gucci, to be in demand,
I think I could be the best in the land.
A photographer, a beautician, I don't have a clue
I need some good guidance to decide what to do.

Ambitions, ambitions what will I pick?
Decisions, decisions they're making me sick
Year Nine, I am only so a few years to go
At the end of my schooling, I'll hopefully know!

Nicola Mayo (13)
St Mary's Grammar School, Magherafelt

Leaves Falling

As I walk out,
And the leaves flutter about,
I look at them prancing and dancing.

They whirl like a fairy,
Glittering and twisting, gracefully.

When they rustle about,
It's as if they're whispering.

They tumble gently down,
From the breeze blowing mildly.

They fall with elegance,
Like snowflakes tumbling down.

They have no life when they have fallen,
Therefore they get crackly and crunchy,
Like thin dried paper.

Then suddenly,
No fluttering about,
As the leaves fall and die out.

Aisling O'Brien (12)
St Mary's Grammar School, Magherafelt

I Heard Nature

As I lay there on the grass,
Wishing that this time would last
And as the warm gentle breeze,
Went all around me so I couldn't freeze.

Then I heard the sound of bees,
Buzzing around in the trees.
Looking for nectar as they go along
And just singing a little song.

Then I heard the song of birds,
Tweet, tweet, tweeting and it turned into words.
As that song faded away,
I heard a little squirrel play.

It jumped about in the trees,
Eating nuts and getting rid of fleas.
Then the breeze blew in the trees
And I heard the sound of rustling leaves.

After a while I got up and thought,
I thought about what I had been taught.
I was taught that there was a lot of nature,
It was a sound once and gone forever.

Nichola McPeake (11)
St Mary's Grammar School, Magherafelt

Clouds

Like balls of soft, white cotton wool,
They float across the sky.
Big white lilies peeking at us,
From a big blue lake.
Like the smoke of a fire
They drift across the sky, dark and gloomy.
They pour water down on us
Like large sponges being *squeezed*
When we look up we see shapes in them,
Faces *smiling* down at us
At sunset when they're orange
Like embers glowing in a grate.
They watch us from above,
With their gleaming cats' eyes.
Just before a storm,
They are tall, grey buildings towering above us.
But sometimes they're yellow,
Like big bunches of lemon roses,
Their petals curling softly in.
They're massive sunlit mountains,
Filling the sky in their glory!

Deirdre Devlin (12)
St Mary's Grammar School, Magherafelt

The Whisper Of Autumn

The whisper of autumn
Weaves its way through the woods
Dancing and prancing
In a jolly old mood.

The whisper of autumn
Gives a content sigh
Like a beautiful swan
It slowly glides by.

The whisper of autumn
Tugs gently at the trees
And slowly, one by one,
Eases off the leaves.

The whisper of autumn
Lets out a lonely wail
But still it flutters gracefully on
Like a twirling, whirling veil.

The whisper of autumn
Holds a note of fear
Too late - it's gone
It won't be back 'til next year.

Amy Higgins (12)
St Mary's Grammar School, Magherafelt

On A Day Like This . . .

The wind wailing like a banshee,
Roaring like a bull that saw red.
Rain and hail knocking at the door
Like a man who locked himself out.
Leaves scuttling like a dog's paws,
Rustling like an animal in a bush.
This is what I hear on a day like this.

Boughs on trees doing the Mexican wave
To show how strong the wind is.
Rain splitting the high heavens
Like someone crying at a funeral.
Leaves playing non-stop games
Struggling to stay on trees.
This is what I hear on a day like this.

Wind is bringing cold
The wind and its icy voice.
Rain is bringing water
It's like it wants to have a water fight.
Leaves feel crisp,
I'm lucky to catch one, no thanks to the wind.

Most people want this weather to go
But I want it to stay.
It is fascinating how it looks, feels and sounds.
These are my thoughts on a day like this.

Cillian Deery (14)
St Mary's Grammar School, Magherafelt

Football

The ball gets thrown up in the air
Players leaping to win possession
Holding the ball as tightly as a clamp
Popping the ball over to a fellow player.

The ball goes wide, keep your head up
There will be another chance for you
Fighting fiercely to win the ball
Look up and kick it over the bar.

Suck in when the attack is coming
Move the ball out faster than light
See space and put it in the corner
Back up the wee corner, forward to get
The score.

Slow down the play when you're ahead
The 45 goes to the full forward
He rattles the net with a super goal
The crowd chant their name
'Ballinderry.'

Point after point shakes the ball catcher
Opposition get a point but no big worry
Ballinderry are in the lead and about to win
They are the champions now and forever.

Karl McKinless (12)
St Mary's Grammar School, Magherafelt

The Roller Coaster

It goes around its track all day,
Swooping and swirling around the corners like a busy bee,
Over the loops and round the twists,
It returns back to the station.

Load it up again,
We all jump on,
We crawl up on the turtle's back,
At the top of the drop, we saw all of Spain,
Falling down the drop, I roared like a lion!

Burning tears came to my eyes like a waterfall,
As the wind flew past like a bird,
There was no time to look around,
We all came back and hopped off,
For the roller coaster to repeat its journey.

Over to the photo booth,
We all roared with laughter,
As we saw how the wind reformed our faces,
We got our notes out,
To buy an embarrassing memory,
Once in a lifetime experience,
Never to be forgotten.

Hannah Cassidy (12)
St Mary's Grammar School, Magherafelt

The Match

The small, white, circular object
Sat on the ground now wanting to move.
Looked up to see a brown thing hurled towards it
Like something it was trying to prove.

Whooossshhh! It hurtled through the air
Like a rocket through the sky.
Sailing, not knowing where to land,
Just watching the world fly by.

Landing. *Thump!* Hard on the blanket of green
Rolling, but before it could stop
The brown monster appeared once again,
Picking it up and causing it to drop.

The monster tried lifting it again
And this time did so successfully.
It made it rest in a huge claw
But it kept bobbing up and down restlessly.

A few seconds later
A sharp blast of noise could be heard.
It was sounded twice more before
The ball was once again dropped like a bird.

It lay there for a couple of minutes
Preparing to take cover,
But not a soul appeared.
The torture was finally over.

Danielle Norton (13)
St Mary's Grammar School, Magherafelt

Hallowe'en

It happened on a Friday night,
Believe me I was there.
The night when all the lights went out,
It gave me such a scare.

First it was the wind;
It howled, whistled and blew.
Then there was the noise
And it was scary too.

The noise was like a wolf,
That was screaming to be free.
It howled and it snarled,
Well, it certainly scared me.

Then it was the lights,
They went out.
It was pitch-black
And I couldn't see.

Then I saw the creature,
with just one hump on its back
And teeth as sharp as razors
And its eyes were black.

It stumbled over to me,
Stretched out its long claws
It laughed a very wicked laugh
And then removed its mask!

Aileen Henry (11)
St Mary's Grammar School, Magherafelt

Winter Wonderland

I looked around me, snow is everywhere!
Glistening beneath the silver sky -
And the little robin sits and stares,
Watching the world pass by.

Icy cobwebs hang from hedges,
Icicles drip from window ledges
And like large statues the trees stand,
Alone in the mist with cold, bare hands.

Snowflakes twirl from the sky,
Falling softly so they can lie.
Animals hibernate and they remain,
Inside till spring comes again.

Inside warm houses, children play,
Opening presents without delay.
Outside they build snowmen in the *white sand,*
Happy to be in this winter wonderland!

The wind howls through every home,
Leaving folk to shiver
And where the fish used to swim,
There's a frozen, icy river.

When I breathe I see my breath,
Floating like a fluffy cloud.
Wrapped up warmly there is no reason,
Why I shouldn't love this season!

Siofra O'Dolan (13)
St Mary's Grammar School, Magherafelt

Forbidden Love

As I wander through the deserted wasteland,
I search for my seed, which has been blown away from our tree,
By the angry wind.
I feel your breath upon my face, but I do not see you,
I feel your footsteps under my footsteps,
But I do not touch you,
You left without a goodbye or a tender kiss.

I keep on running and running like a never-ending rainbow,
Even though I cannot see or find you,
You were my strength, but now I am weak,
You were my soulmate, but now I am lonely,
You were my heart and now that you are gone,
Happiness cannot be pumped around my body.
You left without a goodbye or a tender kiss.

I can remember your soft, ivory skin,
I can remember your wide, blue eyes,
I remember you as I hear your sweet voice in the wind.

It's too late now for destiny has ran out of time.
But, still you left without a goodbye or a tender kiss.

I sit down and curl myself into a ball,
Lying there on the sharp, cold, ground.
My body is shabby and my limbs are numb,
We should have kept our love a divine secret from everyone.
I have hope and faith that someday you will come back to me,
So I will wait
And wait
And wait . . .

Bernadette Kevin (12)
St Mary's Grammar School, Magherafelt

Saved!

Not again, I can't believe it,
Why can't I get out?
The bullies and the back-stabbing
I want to scream and shout.

They hit me for my clothes
My family and my hair
They hit for any stupid thing
It really isn't fair

I hate them all, despise the lot
All the so-called friends
Getting punched and kicked and scratched
For not following their trends

I'll bring the pills up our stairs
And hide them from my mum
I don't think it'll take too long
I hope no one will come

I'm on the bed, I'm getting scared
But I really have to do it.
At least this way, I'll save myself
From every little bit

I'm thinking now, I realise
It's not my time to go
And though this seemed the right idea
This way's better I know

I'll talk to someone, get the bullies caught
So everyone will know
That though they thought this way was right
Bullies can't make you go.

Mark Rocks (12)
St Mary's Grammar School, Magherafelt

Christmas

I love when Christmas is coming,
Everyone is excited and cheerful and bright,
The decorations and Christmas tree,
Shine beautifully with colourful lights.

One Christmas Eve,
One day to go,
Until Christmas Day,
Then we play in the snow.

We open our presents,
Show the gifts to our friends,
We are all so excited,
We hope Christmas never ends!

Then we have our Christmas dinner
And play with another present or two,
Our dinner tastes oh so delicious,
Is that the same with you?

We play all day,
It is so much fun,
Dancing and singing,
It is number one!

What is the most important thing
That happened on Christmas Day?
Baby Jesus was born,
It is the best thing in every way.

When night comes again
And Christmas is away,
We will look back with lovely memories,
Of this very special day.

Ciara Johnston (11)
St Mary's Grammar School, Magherafelt

New Friends

On the first day I was so afraid
That I wouldn't make any new friends,
But when that day was near to a close
I did not want it to end.

My friends like sports and that kind of thing,
But the one thing they hate is the end of lunch,
As the bell goes, *ding, ding, ding.*

Me on the other hand,
I like music and dancing and running and sports.
I always try my best,
Even when I don't come first,
I'm better than all the rest.

We all hang about together,
And are always having a laugh.
We are always there for each other,
When having good days or bad.

We're always sleeping over
At each other's house,
We're good at spreading gossip
And making lots of noise
And we try to make an impression.
On every one of the boys.

My first days are far gone now
And I have many friends.
I don't have worries anymore;
I have nothing to worry about.
We all will be best friends forever,
I'm sure I have no doubt.

Aimee McErlean (11)
St Mary's Grammar School, Magherafelt

What Time Of Year?

The snow fell down in snowflakes,
Like little fluffy clouds falling out of the sky,
So cold but yet so lovely,
The snow fell on the land.

The Christmas tree all covered in white,
The days so dark, not much light,
We know what time of year is coming,
It's one filled with joy, yes it's winter.

The rain bouncing off the rooftops,
I hear its sound, *splash, splash, splash,*
The wind roaring like a bear,
We don't mind. It's winter.

The rain has gone, the snow has fell,
The sun now peeping round the clouds,
What time of year?
I can't really tell.

Sun, rain and snow too,
What time of year? I'm asking you,
Is it summer, winter, autumn or spring?
It's becoming warmer what do you think?

Well I'll tell you once,
Maybe even twice,
And if you're good,
I might tell you thrice.

The season is spring,
Yes, good old spring,
When animals are born and all things grow back,
Renewed, reborn yes that's a fact!

Shauna McAtamney (12)
St Mary's Grammar School, Magherafelt

A Step Too Far

I have witnessed Death, literally,
They say he travels from place to place,
But for three years now, yes, three years running,
From my sight, he hasn't erased.

One year Granny, the next, Grandad,
The two, to me, who meant the most,
To whom my dear, loving mother every Sunday at dinner
Would to both propose a toast.

She'd convey how she missed them tremendously,
And how, crying, she longed for them every night,
She didn't see what I saw next to her, the same presence I
saw beside my grandparents,
Death. It filled me like a jug with fright.

I worried daily from then on,
Like a nervous child on their first visit to the dentist,
Yet this anxiety, this fear, lingered like a yawn.

Four months later at Mum's funeral, they played her favourite song,
For her essence was stripped away, no longer here, it was gone.

That very night, Death reappeared to me,
This was different though, it was just he and I, no one else around,
Usually he'd appear beside those next to die,
My heavy, intense breathing, the only sound . . .

But I realise, months later, as I walk home from school, about to cross
the street
It's been a while since I've seen Death,
How long until the next time we meet?

Anyway, I can't wait to get home, school was boring today,
Teachers are evil, their soul's dark, black as tar,
'Huh! Who honked that horn? Who's calling my name?
Look out for what?' I say, 'What car?'

Too late, Death's reappearance, it was a sign of my death, I was hit
by that car,
Dammit! I missed my sign, and took a step too far.

Brian Quinn (14)
St Mary's Grammar School, Magherafelt

Dancing Dreams

Audience waiting, mouth feeling dry
Tension in movement, too nervous to smile;
Emotions bursting, head crammed with thoughts,
Stage fright kicking in, abusing all my thoughts.
A minute call, body refusing to stay calm.
Bend down to tie my ribbons as my feet distinguish who I am.
Practise one last curtsey, Sal acknowledges me with a bow,
We prepare our opening duo, our chance to shine now.
As we rush onto the stage, greeted by a silent crowd,
Madame's routine I knew so well was nowhere to be found.
Blidned by the lightning which shone so brightly into my eyes,
I struggled to recover the routine I'd forgotten before returning to
my disguise.
Disguised as a graceful swan, gliding across a surface, crystal clear,
When I placed myself in my disguise I was a dancer with elegance
minus fear.
The orchestra, it set the mood, we twrrled and tiptoed around
The stage was a frozen lake, our feet they made no sound.
Our arms outstretched, our heads held high, our passion for dance
will never die.
The lighting was of an icy blue, warmed by my pink leotard and tutu,
Sal looked delightful in his costume of blue,
The stage symbolised my dancing dream coming true,
I was in my element, dancing my best
It was as though I was completing a long awaited quest.
The adrenaline pumped fiercely through each of my veins,
Filling my body full of energy I could not retain.
A sudden leap I had to perform was delivered with style and ease,
The audience responded so enthusiastically it brought us to our knees.
A standing ovation completed my night, filling my ecstatic body full
of delight,
The audience *threw* us flowers all sorts, roses of red and white.
The curtain closed while Sal and I posed, eventually we left
our disguise,
Once again I was myself but the dancer within me remained
in my eyes.

Breige Canavan (14)
St Mary's Grammar School, Magherafelt

Football Crazy

Football is my favourite hobby
I play it every day
I play it in any weather
Nothing gets in my way.

My favourite player is Cristiano Ronaldo
He does a load of tricks
He plays for Man United
And takes their free kicks.

My dad says he'll take me to Old Trafford
And watch Man United
Someday if this dream would come true
I would be so excited.

United are the champions
They've even won the treble,
They've got all the best players
Like Phil and Gary Neville.

United have arch enemies
Their worst is Liverpool
If anyone supported them
I think they would be a fool.

I go training every Monday
And practise all my skills
Kick-ups, step-overs, flicks and balances
And plenty of other thrills.

I have a dream in my head
That someday I'll be a professional
And I will score the crucial goal
In the Champions League final
Lethal Lennon I hear them cheer
And I have a grin from ear to ear.

Aidan Lennon (12)
St Mary's Grammar School, Magherafelt